Find, Hire and Keep
THE
PERFECT
NANNY
A Parent's Guide

This book is dedicated with love to my granddaughters
Emily and Charlotte, with whom I have shared and enjoyed
many special moments.

Love gives naught but itself and takes naught but from itself.
Love possesses not nor would it be possessed;
For love is sufficient unto love.

'The Prophet', Kahlil Gibran

Find, Hire and Keep

THE PERFECT NANNY

A Parent's Guide

Kay Crosse M.A. Cert Ed.

NEW HOLLAND

Published in 2009 by New Holland Publishers (UK) Ltd
London • Cape Town • Sydney • Auckland
www.newhollandpublishers.com

Garfield House
86–88 Edgware Road
London W2 2EA
United Kingdom

80 McKenzie Street
Cape Town 8001
South Africa

Unit 1, 66 Gibbes Street
Chatswood
NSW 2067
Australia

218 Lake Road
Northcote, Auckland
New Zealand

ISBN 978 1 84773 173 9

Senior Editor: Kate Parker
Production: Melanie Dowland
Design concept: Bill Mason
Cover design and design: Ian Hughes, Mousemat Design Ltd
DTP: Peter Gwyer
Editorial direction: Rosemary Wilkinson

1 2 3 4 5 6 7 8 9 10

Reproduction by Pica Digital Pte. Ltd., Singapore
Printed and bound in India by Replika Press

Note: The author and publishers have made every effort to ensure that the information
given in this book is safe and accurate, but they cannot accept liability for any
resulting injury or loss or damage to either property or person, whether direct or
consequential and howsoever arising.

CONTENTS

INTRODUCTION 6

CHAPTER 1
FINDING YOUR WAY THROUGH THE CHILDCARE MAZE 8

CHAPTER 2
THE NANNY SEARCH 26

CHAPTER 3
HOW TO INTERVIEW AND SELECT THE PERFECT NANNY 42

CHAPTER 4
EMPLOYER RESPONSIBILITIES 64

CHAPTER 5
NANNY MANAGEMENT 72

CHAPTER 6
THE NANNY'S PERSPECTIVE 94

CHAPTER 7
EARLY YEARS EDUCATION IN THE HOME 104

CHAPTER 8
SPECIALIST NANNIES FOR SPECIAL SITUATIONS 118

USEFUL SOURCES 136

INDEX 139

INTRODUCTION

P arents choose to employ a nanny for many reasons, but the most likely is to provide reliable childcare for young children whose parents are in full-time employment. Today, the main reason for the increase in families wanting to employ a nanny is that more women are working than ever before. However, finding good-quality childcare is a complex and time-consuming job, and so this book has been written to help parents find their way through the childcare maze.

Parents can choose from different forms of childcare, including day nurseries and childminders, but more and more parents are choosing to employ a nanny. This is because the child benefits from being cared for in his or her own home and, increasingly, there is economic sense in employing a nanny when there is more than one child in the family. In addition, parents who work irregular hours or who have to stay away from home occasionally value the fact that their resident nanny will be on hand to cope with these situations.

It is difficult for parents looking for childcare for the first time to know the sort of person who would be the perfect carer for their family situation. At the top of the list must be someone who will keep the child safe at all times. However, not all nannies are qualified and not all nannies are registered or have undergone checks that could provide reassurance for parents. This book will, among many other things, help parents find out more about relevant childcare qualifications and inform them about how to make pre-employment checks to keep their child safe.

The majority of nannies are female, but increasingly men are choosing to work as nannies. Male nannies can provide excellent support to families and be well suited to the care of young children in the private home, bringing new experiences into the lives of the children. The basis on which a modern-day nanny works is also changing; for example, a nanny can be resident, or travel daily to the family home or be part of a nanny-share between two families.

This book considers all aspects of finding the perfect nanny, guiding parents through the recruitment and selection phase to the very important aspect of how to keep your perfect nanny. Advice is given regarding some of the pitfalls likely to occur, together with ways of keeping communication channels open, while practical help is offered through consideration of an employer's responsibilities. For many parents, employing a nanny is their first experience of being an employer and, therefore, they are not always aware of what this involves. Keeping a nanny is as important as finding one and this book provides an insight into the nanny's perspective. An employer who is aware of what it is like to be a nanny working in a private family is an employer who will be able to make adjustments that may result in a happy nanny who wants to stay with a particular family for a long time. Nanny Management (*page 72*) provides tips for the employer on maintaining an effective employer/employee relationship; while Specialist Nannies for Special Situations (*page 118*) examines particular family situations and the best sort of nanny to employ in these circumstances.

Your perfect nanny is likely to be well-qualified and experienced but, above all, he or she should have a genuine love of children and enjoy their company. Charlotte Zeepvat in her book *From Cradle to Crown* informs us that the young Prince Berthold of Baden had an English nanny, and when he was asked what his name was he replied, 'In German my name is Berthold. In English my names are "sweetheart" and "darling".' It is this deep-seated love and respect for children that a perfect nanny will bring to your family, and after a few months you will wonder how you and your family ever managed before!

CHAPTER 1

FINDING YOUR WAY THROUGH THE CHILDCARE MAZE

Parents considering how to provide childcare for their children face a wide range of options. They have to negotiate their way through a significant amount of information, listen to many anecdotal stories and then try to make the correct and most appropriate choice of childcare for their own individual circumstances. This chapter outlines the choices available to parents and considers the merits of each option.

Each family situation is different and whatever the choice made it should be as appropriate as possible for the ages of the children and meet their needs and those of the parents. In this chapter parents will find information on:

8

- *Identifying the needs of the family*
- *Support for parents*
- *Childcare alternatives to employing a nanny*
- *Is the nanny option the best for your family?*

IDENTIFYING THE NEEDS OF THE FAMILY

There are many different types of family and family lifestyles. Each family will have its own special requirements for childcare arrangements. It is no longer true to describe the 'nuclear' family with two parents and two children and grandparents living close by as the typical set-up. Today, changes in lifestyle and cultural expectations, as well as increased ethnic diversity, are reflected in increased variety in family structures.

Parents need to identify their family priorities before starting their childcare search. Each parent will have his or her own perspective on what constitutes good childcare for their children, and it is helpful for parents to agree their priorities and to say why these priorities are important to them. Traditionally, the mother has taken primary responsibility for childcare decisions but there is an increasing and welcome desire by many fathers to be involved in these important decisions.

Family requirements will change according to the ages and number of children. Most childcare is needed for children under the age of five years, in the time before they start formal education. However, older children also have to be considered as they may require childcare before and after school and in school holidays. Childcare that is affordable for one child in the family may cease to be appropriate or affordable when a second or third child is born. When trying to identify particular requirements, the following points are some of the initial thoughts for parents to take into account:

9

WHAT ARE THE CHILDCARE NEEDS OF YOUR FAMILY?

- Is childcare required because you are working or need time for your own study or other activities?

- What hours will you require childcare for?
- Do you need full-time or part-time childcare?

continued on next page

- How flexible do you need your childcare provision to be?
- Do you want childcare in a home-based or group situation?
- Do you work from home and require 'peace and quiet' in which to work?
- Do you have room in your home to accommodate a resident nanny?
- Do you want the children to have one or more carers?
- Would you like all your children to be looked after in one location?

- Do you need a 'special' carer for a child who has a special need, such as a disability?
- Would you like your children to be able to take part in activities, such as swimming or shopping?
- What does your budget allow you to consider in choosing childcare?
- What 'emergency backup' is there for when the carer is ill or away on holiday?
- How important are the carer's qualifications and experience to you?

The answers to these questions, which will be further considered in later chapters of this book, will determine the direction of any fact-finding mission. Whatever the final decision, parents must be confident that the chosen provision is one that they trust, offers childcare that is totally safe and where their children will be happy.

True life stories: A time and a place

Mr and Mrs W were looking forward to the birth of their first child. Mrs W knew that she wanted to return to work after taking her maternity leave. From the experiences of her friends she also knew that making arrangements for childcare could take a long time. This was new territory for both her and her husband, and they spent many weeks researching and thinking about the various options. After several weeks, they both decided that they wanted to employ a nanny. This decision was mainly based on the fact that they both worked quite far from home and that the time they would arrive home each evening could be very varied. They also knew that their home could be easily *adapted to be comfortable for a resident nanny yet still enable all parties to 'have their own space'. The next decision they made was to approach an agency to help them in their search.*

Having considered some of the important issues of childcare provision, the practicalities have to be addressed; these are mainly connected with what is available in any particular area at an affordable price. Leave plenty of time for research and to allow for waiting lists. A helpful starting point in gathering information is to contact your local authority's Children's Information Service (*see* Useful Sources *on page 156*), which will have a list of the names and addresses of all childcare services available in your area. This list is regularly updated and registered childcarers and locations will be checked by the Office for Standards in Education (Ofsted). Since April 2008, each local authority has to ensure that there is a sufficiency of childcare for working parents; the Children's Information Service also offers a one-to-one service for parents to explain the choices available and to identify an appropriate choice.

SUPPORT FOR PARENTS

In the UK, there has been a recent emphasis on improving the provision of childcare and supporting parents in balancing family and work responsibilities. This approach is outlined in the government's National Childcare Strategy. The government has expanded the number of childcare places and put in place measures to improve the quality of early years services. The establishing of the Children's Information Service is part of this improvement, as is an entitlement for three- and four-year old children to free, part-time early years education, checking of suitability of childcarers and an increase of childcare availability to more than 1.2 million registered places.

In 1998 the government published a paper 'Meeting the Childcare Challenge' to outline its national strategy to get childcare right for all children and to give parents genuine choice whether they look after children full-time or combine work, education or training with parenting.

THE KEY POINTS OF THE NATIONAL CHILDCARE STRATEGY ARE:

* Quality of childcare
* Affordability of childcare
* Registered childcare
* Accessibility of childcare
* Developing partnerships

QUALITY OF CHILDCARE

Since 1971, the proportion of working mothers has increased from 56 per cent to currently more than 70 per cent. More fathers are undertaking home responsibilities and many single parents work and look after their children. There are significant implications for society and for families where large numbers of babies and very young children share their care and early education with adults other than their parents.

It is imperative that childcare provision is responsive to the needs of the individual child and is of the very highest quality. It is not enough for there to be more and more childcare places available, the increased provision has to be able to 'tune into' individual children and enable them to reach their full potential.

Parents want childcare that enables their children to be safe and happy, and they want quality childcare; the challenge is how to make this happen. There has been rigorous debate about what is meant by quality. At the heart of good-quality childcare is the warm and loving interaction between the adult and the child. This is what parents need to observe in their chosen childcarer.

The awarding body the Council for Awards in Children's Care and Education (CACHE) has a framework for the values and principles for those who undertake its qualifications. This framework clearly sets out how a competent carer should approach his or her work and it is helpful for parents to consider their own priorities within some of the CACHE guidelines:

COUNCIL FOR AWARDS IN CHILDREN'S CARE AND EDUCATION (CACHE) GUIDELINES
(FOUND IN ALL CACHE COURSE HANDBOOKS)

Childcare practitioners must ensure that they put the child first by:

- ensuring the child's welfare
- showing compassion and sensitivity
- respecting the child as an individual
- upholding the child's rights and dignity
- enabling the child to reach their full potential
- never using physical punishment
- respecting the parent as the primary carer and educator of the child
- respecting the customs, values and spiritual beliefs of the child and their family
- honouring the confidentiality of information relating to the child and their family, unless its disclosure is required by law or in the best interest of the child

AFFORDABILITY OF CHILDCARE

Many parents are concerned about the affordability of childcare and their budget will determine in part what options are open to them. Financial considerations are changeable, too, as what is affordable for one child may become not so affordable if a sibling is born. This is particularly the case with group childcare, although some nurseries have slightly reduced fees for the second and subsequent child. There are some sources of financial advice including the HM Revenue and Customs (HMRC) Tax Credit Helpline. Many families are eligible for financial help. The amount payable changes as the family circumstances change, so it is important to inform the Tax Credit Office of these changes. Working Tax Credit (WTC) helps with childcare costs for low- and middle-income families and is paid directly into a bank account. Extra help is available to working

13

parents through a childcare element of the WTC. The purpose of the additional payment is to help with childcare costs. Parents can claim back a significant percentage of their childcare costs, up to certain limits, when their child is cared for by a registered or approved childcarer. There are eligibility restrictions, however, and parents should check these with HMRC.

Child Tax Credit (CTC) is paid to families with an income of currently less than £58,000 (or £66,000 if there is at least one child under one year old). The maximum CTC child element is approximately £32 a week for each child, with extra help available for families with a child who is disabled. This amount is paid directly into a bank account and is in addition to the Child Benefit payment.

Parents with children aged three and four who attend nursery schools or classes in the state sector do not pay any fees. This is also the case for children of the same age who attend pre-schools. Privately run establishments charge fees, which will vary from school to school. Parents need to remember that some nursery and pre-school establishments do not always open for the hours that a working parent might require, so this type of setting may have to be combined with childcare at another setting, such as a childminder.

An increasing number of employers offer support to their employees for their childcare costs in the form of Childcare Vouchers, usually in exchange for a reduction in salary. Some of the financial value of the Childcare Voucher is exempt from both income tax and National Insurance contributions as long as the voucher is used to pay for registered or approved childcare. If a parent decides to accept childcare vouchers from his or her employer this can affect any entitlement to tax credits, so this needs to be carefully investigated.

REGISTERED CHILDCARE

Not all types of childcare need to be registered. Care for children aged eight years and over, hotel-based babysitting, and short-term occasional care operating for less than six days a year, activity-based care and care provided by nannies (unless they look after the children of more than two families) does not need to be registered.

However, these types of provision can be registered on the voluntary part of the Ofsted Childcare Register (OCR) if they meet the requirements with regard to their people, premises and provision. The benefits for parents choosing childcare appearing on this register are the availability of financial benefits and the knowledge that staff will have been checked against the Criminal Records Bureau (CRB) enhanced check. This enhanced check means that at the time of the check the person does not have a criminal record and is considered a suitable person to have unsupervised access to the children in their care. In addition to the CRB check, Ofsted will also carry out checks on the person mainly responsible for childcare, such as the childminder or manager of the day nursery. These include checks with each social services department where the person has lived for the last five years and a medical report from the person's GP. Care that is voluntarily registered will be inspected by Ofsted from time to time or following a complaint. Ofsted will notify the providers of the results of the inspection but will not produce a report. If parents choose to use unregistered childcare they need to be especially careful to check that the provider has had a CRB check.

Childcare that is registered by Ofsted includes:
• People who provide day care for children under eight years of age for more than two hours each day
• People who work as registered childminders
• Nursery education settings that are on the local authorities list to provide free places for three- and four-year-old children

These childcare services are checked by Ofsted before they are registered. They are inspected regularly to ensure that the appropriate national standards are met relating to the suitability of the person, health and safety, equipment and the care, learning and play that the services deliver. Ofsted provides reports after its inspection and these can be read by parents on the Ofsted website (*see* Useful Sources *on page 136*). These reports, although very helpful to parents, should not take the place of a personal visit and a full

15

discussion with the provider. All registered providers have a certificate of registration, which they are required to display. Parents can also phone Ofsted to check a registration.

ACCESSIBILITY OF CHILDCARE

Accessibility of childcare will vary from area to area – often there are several day nurseries in one neighbourhood and few childminders, in other areas it may be the opposite. Where parents choose to employ a resident nanny, they often have a choice that is not restricted by local demand. Some parents choose childcare that is convenient for their workplace or home. Choosing childcare for convenience, while very tempting and understandable, is not a criterion that should replace those connected with quality. Choosing on the convenience criterion can very often result in childcare that may be unsatisfactory and short-lived; this then means further change for children and parents, which is unsettling and upsetting.

DEVELOPING PARTNERSHIPS

Working in partnership with parents is another key factor of quality childcare. A strong partnership between the parents and the nanny allows effective communication to take place. Good partnerships between professional agencies connected with health, education and social services often mean that parents can access support for their children and family more easily. When real partnership is in place, children benefit by having consistency and security.

CHILDCARE ALTERNATIVES TO EMPLOYING A NANNY

- Day nurseries
- Children's centres
- Nursery school and nursery classes
- Pre-schools
- Out-of-school childcare
- Childminders
- Au pairs

One of the initial considerations for parents is whether or not they want their child cared for in a group setting outside of their home. If this is their choice then day-care and children's centres offer full-time or part-time provision, and nursery school and pre-schools provide part-time care and education during term time. Out-of-school childcare by its very nature offers before and after school provision in term time and full-time care during the summer holidays. By 2010, the government wants all schools to provide a range of extended services throughout the country. The plan, laid out in the government's Ten Year Childcare Strategy, is to offer to parents and their children 'wrap around childcare from 8am to 6pm either on the school campus or in collaboration with a group of providers on a shared site, if necessary with supervised transport arrangements'. Although this would help parents with childcare during holidays and after school, it is important to consider whether such long absences from home and parents are best suited to the child's individual needs.

Care and education in a home-based setting for either a very small number of children or for a single child can be provided by a childminder in his or her own home or a nanny or au pair in the child's home.

DAY NURSERIES
What the service offers
Day nurseries provide care and education for children between the ages of six weeks and five years. They can be operated by the local authority, on behalf of an employer, privately run or organised by a national chain of day nurseries. Opening times vary but some nurseries are open from 7am to 7pm and most are open for 50 weeks each year. Children can attend on a full- or part-time basis. Children will mostly be cared for in groups of their own age and nurseries have to have sufficient staff to satisfy the national standards with regard to adult/child ratios. These dictate that there should be one adult for every three children under two years of age, one adult for every four children aged from two to three years and one adult for every eight children aged from three to five years.

Day nurseries are organised to provide childcare even when particular staff are ill or on leave. They will have qualified staff working as early years practitioners as well as some unqualified staff working as nursery assistants, who may also be undertaking some initial qualifications.

Remember to make several visits at different times of the day when deciding on the choice of childcare, and carefully observe the way in which the staff interact with the children. Look to see if both look happy, if conversation between adults and children is plentiful, and if there is ample room for play with an outdoor area easily available to the children. Call the National Day Nurseries Association for further information (*see* Useful Sources *on page 136*).

Special considerations
It is particularly important to be aware of how establishments satisfactorily staff their nurseries at the beginning and the end of each day, as these can be demanding times for staff and unsettling times for anxious or tired children. Although in practice there tend not to be very young babies in nurseries, due in part to the availability of parental leave, it is absolutely essential to ensure that the care and education offered to very young babies is responsive to their needs. This includes each baby having a key person to help them settle in and to ensure that his or her individual needs with respect to rest, sleep, play and feeding can be accommodated.

CHILDREN'S CENTRES
What the service offers
Children's Centres are closely linked with the government's Sure Start programme (designed to support families through health and education provision) and offer a range of services to children and families. Services are organised to be easily accessible to parents and to support them in all aspects of looking after their children, as well as helping them to obtain work or take up studying for new qualifications. People can also use a Children's Centre if they are pregnant or are a parent or carer of a child under five years of age.

In a Children's Centre all early years provision, including early learning and care, will be inspected by Ofsted. Many centres are open for 48 weeks each year, five days a week, for about ten hours each day. Staff are qualified and usually come from a range of education, health and social services backgrounds. Find out more from the Sure Start website (*see* Useful Sources *on page 136*).

Special considerations

A very real benefit of Children's Centres is that full-time care is provided and parents can find a range of services in one place that can provide them with support from pregnancy until their child is five years old. Increasingly, centres offer out-of-school and after-school provision.

NURSERY SCHOOL AND NURSERY CLASSES

What the service offers

Nursery schools and classes offer early education and care for children between three and five years of age. Some are part of the state education system and others are run by the private and voluntary sector. They are open between 9am and 3pm in term time and children usually start by attending for half-day sessions and may then progress to a full day. They are inspected by Ofsted and the staff team may consist of a qualified teacher, nursery nurse or learning support assistant. Very often a nursery class will be part of a primary school – this helps the children when they begin formal schooling at five as they will know the school and perhaps some of the staff.

Special considerations

If parents are working full time then it may appear that this option is not a practical one. However, it can often be used in combination with a childminder, employed to look after your child before and after school, often in the company of other children. In this way, the child has opportunities for socialising and learning, and the childminder's home will provide a welcome change of environment and source of alternate activities.

PRE-SCHOOLS

What the service offers

Pre-schools developed from the playgroup movement started in the 1960s. Pre-school offers early years education to children aged from three to five, although some groups will accept children from two years. Initially, pre-schools were led and run by parents, not all of whom would have had early years qualifications. More recently, many of the staff are qualified and offer the children extensive learning experiences through play and creative activities. The staff consistently promote development, especially social and emotional development. In many pre-schools, parents help on a rota basis during sessions or provide support in other ways. Sessions last approximately three hours during term time for each day of the week or in some cases for just two or three days a week. Children can initially attend part time and then build up to five sessions. This service can be combined with a childminder if the hours are insufficient. Some playgroups are now extending their services to full-day care. A registered pre-school is inspected by Ofsted.

Special considerations

If the local schools accept children before their fifth birthday, many children will go to school as a 'rising five'. In this case, try to decide if your child is ready for the more formal environment of school or if there is a benefit for them in remaining for another term at his or her pre-school. Remember that a great deal of learning can take place through play and that the smaller group size and more informal setting can promote all aspects of a child's development. Remember to put your child's name on any waiting list as early as possible as some pre-schools are very popular.

OUT-OF-SCHOOL CHILDCARE

What the service offers

This service will offer a range of provision, including breakfast clubs open from about 8am and after-school clubs opening from the close of school to about 6pm. Holiday play schemes open during school holidays usually from 8am to 6pm. Parents can choose from a combination of these services according to their need. Many schools now organise these services on the school site, but they are also run by nurseries, sports centres, or voluntary and private providers. Staff may be trained playworkers or be led by people who have other relevant qualifications. Most out-of-school groups look after children aged five to eleven years. Groups who have children aged over eight years do not have to be registered or inspected by Ofsted.

Special considerations
Some groups enable children from one family to attend the same group, which is both enjoyable for the children and more convenient for the parents. A balance of home and out-of-school activities during school holidays gives children the opportunity to amuse themselves, follow their own interests, organise their own time and play with their own friends.

CHILDMINDERS
What the service offers
Registered childminders are professional carers who choose to look after other people's children, sometimes with their own children, in their own home. Childminders are self-employed and can usually offer some flexibility in terms of childcare hours. They will agree a contract with parents to cover hours of childcare, cost and what is paid during holidays and if the childminder or child is ill. When registered, the childminder will have had checks carried out with regard to references, training, Criminal Record Bureau enhanced checks and health checks. The members of his or her family over 18 years of age will also have had Criminal Record Bureau checks carried out. A childminder's home will have been checked to ensure that it is a safe and suitable environment for young children. Parents should also check that the childminder has public liability insurance and that the garden, play and sleeping areas have been insured and inspected. All childminders in England and Wales are required to have carried out a basic registration course, including first-aid training.

21

A childminder can look after children of any age, including babies. Regulations state that a childminder can look after six children under the age of eight years. Of those six children, no more than three children should be under the age of five years. Of those three children, no more than one child should be under 12 months, although exceptions can be made for siblings. Childminders will often collect children from school and pre-school.

Special considerations

Choosing a childminder will enable children to be cared for in a home-based setting. Childminders will take children on everyday outings that parents would choose to do with their own children. Many childminders are qualified with relevant early years qualifications. They have often worked in group care settings and have become a childminder so that they can both work and stay at home to care for their own children. Many are keen to extend their professional knowledge and undertake further training. A close relationship often forms between parents and childminder as they usually meet on a daily basis.

AU PAIRS

What the service offers

Au pairs most often come to this country as part of a cultural exchange programme. Their duties include childcare and 'light' housework. They will usually expect to be able to attend language classes on a part-time basis. An au pair who comes from a country within the European Union (EU) may work for up to 30 hours each week, plus two evenings' babysitting; whereas an au pair from a non-EU country can work for 25 hours per week, plus two evenings' baby sitting. There are many agencies who will offer to arrange an au pair placement for a family. It is not only important to check out what services the agency offers and to use local knowledge to check its reputation, it is also best to find out exactly what checks the agency carries out on the au pairs it is seeking to place. Au pairs often wish to live as part of a family and may have improving their language skills and travelling at the top of their priority list. This may mean that childcare is their means to these ends. Au pairs can work legally if they fulfil certain requirements:

WHAT DEFINES AN AU PAIR?

- A single person between the ages of 17 and 25 who wishes to come to the UK to learn English
- A person who stays for up to two years as a member of an English-speaking family

- Help is provided in the home for up to five hours each day
- At least two days a week are given as time off
- A minimum allowance of £55 per week is provided

Some au pairs require a visa and information about this can be found on the Home Office Border and Immigration website – www.workingintheuk.gov.uk.

Special considerations
Au pairs may or may not have childcare qualifications or experience. Parents or agency staff may not be able to meet the au pair for an interview before the post is taken up, although it may be possible to have telephone and email contact. Parents need to be clear about the responsibilities given to the au pair and also be realistic as to the amount of supervision, guidance and support required. A very simple written explanation of the duties and the daily family schedule is very helpful. Leave clear written instructions about what to do in the case of a household or childcare emergency, together with a phone number of an adult who can provide emergency support at short notice. It is inappropriate and inadvisable to assume that an au pair will be knowledgeable about childcare and understand the safety issues surrounding babies and very young children. This needs to be sensitively explored so that expectations

23

on both sides are realistic. Parents also need to understand that the au pair may need a lot of support when first arriving in a foreign country and learning a new language.

IS THE NANNY OPTION THE BEST FOR YOUR FAMILY?

What the service provides

The perfect nanny will offer you flexibility when you have to work longer hours and will also provide an excellent foundation for your children in terms of their care and education. The family will, therefore, have a warm, reliable and supportive framework within which to bring up children. There is a range of agencies keen to place their nannies with families.

Nannies provide childcare usually in the home of their employer. Some employers decide to share a nanny, in which case the children are cared for in a home setting but not necessarily in their own home. Parents must be prepared to take on the legal and financial responsibilities of being an employer. Nannies may not have any qualifications but plentiful experience instead, while others may be both highly qualified and experienced. Nannies working in the child's home do not have to be registered with Ofsted, but they can be on the voluntary part of the register if they meet the basic requirements.

Parents can choose to employ a nanny on a daily basis or on a residential basis if they have sufficient accommodation. Without a doubt, a residential nanny provides most flexibility in terms of childcare and can cope when a parent is unexpectedly late home from work or is required to be away from home for a few days.

Nannies are usually expected to undertake all of the duties connected with the care and education of the children and, if qualified, can be expected to be knowledgeable and skilled childcarers. They undertake household duties connected with the care of the children, such as the children's meals and laundry. Parents need to be very explicit as to their expectations. Nannies look after all of the children in the family during the day and, if necessary, both before and after school and in the holidays.

24

If resident, they usually work from 7am to 7pm each day with two days off each week. Non-resident nannies also work quite long hours to support working parents.

True life stories: Number two on the way

Sarah and James were expecting their second baby. Their eldest daughter, Charlotte, would be four years old when the baby was born. Charlotte had happily attended a local day nursery, but Sarah was not convinced that this would be the right childcare option when there were two children. Sarah had decided that she would take her full maternity leave and that Charlotte would either reduce her attendance at her day nursery or perhaps start at a pre-school for just the mornings. Sarah was looking forward to being at home and to spending more time with Charlotte. James suggested that they employ a nanny who would be able to help Sarah look after their baby and also take Charlotte to pre-school when Sarah returned to work. They decided that they would advertise for a nanny who had some baby experience and who also had an interest in creative and other learning activities that Charlotte would enjoy.

Special considerations

If the children are at school, parents need to be clear as to what duties are expected to be completed during the school hours. Some employers agree to some of these hours being spent helping in their child's pre-school or nursery school or being used for study. Some nannies like to specialise in caring for children with special needs and in doing so provide excellent care for the child and support for the whole family. Some employers provide extra 'perks' with the job, such as gym membership or private use of the nanny car. However, parents need to ascertain that the nanny is attracted to the job for professional reasons and not for the attractive 'perks'.

As you read further, you will find many more subjects to discuss during the nanny interview. Decide on topics that are most relevant to your family and add others that are important to you personally.

CHAPTER 2

THE NANNY SEARCH

Once parents have decided to employ a nanny they are then faced with the task of finding the right nanny for their family circumstances and lifestyle. This chapter outlines points to consider in the 'nanny search'. Issues regarding the drawing up of an accurate job description are discussed, together with the ways in which this can be supportive to both employers and employees.

In this chapter, parents will find information on:

- *Choosing the right carer for the family*
- *Understanding early years qualifications*
- *The nanny search*

CHOOSING THE RIGHT CARER FOR THE FAMILY

Making the right choice is every parent's wish. Where the relationship is a happy and professional one it tends to last for a long time and everybody benefits. The relationship between a nanny and an employer is an unusual one as the work takes place in the employer's home and there is some overlap between professional and personal lives, particularly in the case of a resident nanny.

The role of a nanny will vary from family to family and will depend on whether the post is carried out in a formal or informal way.

WHICH NANNY?

- A daily nanny
- A resident nanny
- A maternity nanny to provide short-term care for a newborn baby and mother
- A temporary nanny to help with a family emergency
- A nanny to share between two families

FORMAL OR INFORMAL?

Nanny positions can be described as 'informal' or 'formal'. An informal post can mean that the nanny is thought of as part of the family; has meals with them and can be asked to carry out some non-nursery duties, such as cleaning out the guinea-pig hutch, taking the dog for a walk, doing some cleaning and collecting the dry cleaning.

In a formal post, the role of the nanny is more clearly defined and there may be other household staff employed too. In this situation it is important for the employer to be clear as to 'who does what'. If there are staff employed to clean the house and do the laundry is the nanny expected to clean the children's and the nanny's rooms and do the children's laundry? Parents are advised to make very clear 'who does what and when'. The nanny working in a formal role for a family may be expected to wear a uniform for all or part of her work. The uniform may be specified by the parents or a nanny may be asked to wear the uniform of the college from where the original qualification was achieved.

True life stories: Mary Poppins

Vicki was looking forward to her first interview for a nanny post in London. She felt that the post was just right for her and that she had the appropriate experience. Her college qualification had given her a level of knowledge and skill that meant she was well prepared for the interview. However, she was a little anxious as this would be the first time that she might work for an American family. The mother, an actress, was interested to know that she had worn a uniform during her training and asked that she wore it to the interview. Vicki ensured that she was smartly and correctly dressed in her uniform, and she felt that it gave her a little more confidence. She was amazed and delighted when the door opened and she was warmly welcomed with 'Wow, you really are Mary Poppins!'. The interview went very well, and when the job was offered to her she readily accepted the post. Her employer was impressed not only by her appearance but also by her childcare knowledge. She did, however, tell Vicki that she would not be required to wear her uniform when working as their nanny as she thought that this would make her and her child rather conspicuous.

SOLE CHARGE OR SHARED CARE?

If a nanny job is described as 'sole charge' there will be an expectation on the part of the nanny that she will usually be able to organise her day with the children more or less as she decides. The nanny will like to have a well-planned and predictable day, making sure there is time to take children to and from nursery or school and also to cook the children's meals and do their laundry. She will have a large amount of responsibility and employers have to be certain that the nanny will be competent in this situation. A sole charge post does not mean, however, that parents do not play a full part in decision-making and have full involvement as to how their children's day is organised. The level of involvement that a parent may have is a potential area for conflict and requires sensitive yet firm handling on the part of the employer.

A 'shared care' post is offered when a parent wants to spend time with his or her children but also wants to be able to spend time away from home knowing that the children are being well cared for. 'Shared care' can also describe a post where there are many children in one family and the parent wants to have someone who is capable and trusted to share the upbringing of the children and the various domestic duties connected with looking after young children. It is essential in this type of post to discuss and adopt a common approach to the children's care as children will often try to 'divide and conquer' and to play the parent off against the nanny and vice versa. Showing a united front is vital in this type of situation.

PERSONAL QUALITIES

There is much work to be done before arriving at the correct choice of carer. It is worth spending some time identifying and discussing what sort of person you like meeting and inviting into your home. Although the appointment is a professional rather than a personal one, it makes sense to consider the candidates in both lights, as the nanny will be in your house for many hours and, even more importantly, will be spending a great deal of time with your children.

Personal characteristics can gain increasing importance the longer the nanny remains with a family. Some parents are happy to have a talkative, outgoing person around them and enjoy his or her constant chatter and lively nature. Others prefer a quiet, reflective person who gets on with his or her work competently in a calm and unobtrusive manner. In reality, someone who can express all of these characteristics at the appropriate times may be ideal for most parents. Think about what is best for you, and when you conduct first and second interviews try to imagine having the nanny around your home for a long time. Does this imbue you with optimism and enthusiasm or with a slight sense of doubt?

This is a time to trust your instincts and to pursue those applications about which you feel positive. You are making a very important decision and it requires a combination of 'gut instinct' and considered judgement about a person's professional competency. You need to feel that you will like your nanny as well as have complete trust in his or her knowledge and skills. If you do not have these feelings, be prepared to start your search again. It is important to take sufficient time to know that you will enjoy the company of your nanny and that your children will be warmly looked after and have many fun and enjoyable times.

Some employers think that their ideal nanny needs to have the following personal qualities, which are listed in no particular order of preference:

THE PERFECT NANNY'S PERSONAL QUALITIES

- Caring
- Adaptable
- Ability to 'tune into' children
- Cheerful
- Warm and loving
- Reliable
- Creative

- Honest
- Trustworthy
- Punctual
- Patient
- Well-presented
- Common sense
- A good communicator

When making your own list it is important to think about the needs of your children. To a certain extent the age of the children can initially lead parents towards thinking about particular qualities, such as wanting a warm-hearted, sensitive and gentle nanny if there is a newborn in their family. Other parents may think that an outgoing, physically active nanny is needed as they have three-year-old boy twins. These are short-term criteria on which to base a decision as the baby will grow up and the twin boys will need a sensitive and gentle nanny for those times when they do not want to run around the garden, but instead need someone to understand that they may have a few difficulties settling into their new pre-school, for example. In this respect, adaptability and the ability to 'tune into' children jump to near the top of any list.

In many ways, dividing personal and professional qualities when looking for a nanny is artificial, as it is the personal qualities that enable the professional skills and knowledge to be perfected through training and experience. The very best nannies have these personal qualities in part when they begin their qualification. Good training brings out the best in the nannies, and as experience and knowledge is gained they can offer the very best in care and education to children and real support to families. A good nanny is often described as a life-support system to a family; in many ways this is the reality, as the way in which children are cared for affects the whole family. When the children and nanny are happy, parents can go to work and organise their lives to the benefit of everyone.

When carrying out interviews for people who wish to train as early years professionals, many of the personal qualities previously listed are those that the interviewers are looking for, as when these are present it makes the possibility of training a good practitioner more likely.

UNDERSTANDING EARLY YEARS QUALIFICATIONS

There is a wide range of early years qualifications at various levels. These levels indicate, in part, the amount of responsibility that the holder of the qualification can reasonably be expected to be given. Diplomas are awarded at Level 3 and Certificates indicate a Level 2 award. A Level 3 award is considered to be equivalent to an 'A-level' qualification and generally takes two years to complete on a full-time basis. Courses provide the necessary skills and knowledge to be a competent childcare worker and contain a significant amount of practical childcare experience. Although a nanny need not have any qualification to undertake the role, it is definitely recommended that a nanny does have an appropriate qualification. Where early years practitioners have a Level 3 qualification the employer should be confident in knowing that they can work safely and competently in a situation that is unsupervised; this is important, as nannies will work for most of their time in a private home where there is no direct supervision. Holders of Level 2 qualifications should have supervision and are likely to work in a day nursery where they can be supported to progress to taking Level 3 qualifications.

LEVEL 3 QUALIFICATIONS – WHAT TO LOOK FOR

All Level 3 qualifications will have a curriculum that enables the student to understand a young child's physical, social, emotional, language and cognitive development. Learners will also study the care of children who are ill, the demands of employment, ways in which to offer all children equality of opportunity and ways of responding to children's individual needs.

CACHE Diploma in Child Care and Education

Probably the most widely known of the Level 3 qualifications are those awarded by the Council for Awards in Children's Care and Education (CACHE) This awarding body is a specialist organisation offering qualifications connected with early years and children's care, education and playwork.

Parents who employ a very experienced nanny may employ someone with an NNEB, a qualification that was offered by the early forerunner of CACHE – the National Nursery Examination Board. This qualification was respected and trusted by employers and has as its successor the Diploma in Child Care and Education. It is this diploma that most parents will encounter on a nanny's CV as it is widely held by many practitioners. A more recent qualification offered by CACHE is the Diploma in Home-based Childcare, which, as its name suggests, has an emphasis on learning how to care for children in the private home; these practitioners will be employed as nannies or childminders.

BTEC National Diploma in Nursery Nursing
The BTEC National Diploma in Nursery Nursing, although offered by a different awarding body, has a similar curriculum to that of the CACHE diploma, combining both academic and practical activities. Both awarding bodies expect their Level 3 candidates to have a range of practical experience, including that of day nurseries, pre-schools and nursery schools; but these candidates may not have had training placements in the private home.

National Vocational Qualifications
National Vocational Qualifications (NVQs) are usually undertaken by people who are already working as early years practitioners and who wish to accredit their experience formally and gain further knowledge through obtaining their NVQ. These qualifications can be studied in college but are also offered by training providers. There is normally more emphasis on practical experience, but all students must have the relevant childcare knowledge.

The Norland Diploma
There are now only two private colleges training early years practitioners, Norland College and Chiltern College. Norland College, a private college located in the city of Bath in Somerset, specialises in training very professional early years practitioners, the majority of whom choose to work as nannies in private homes. The author of this book worked at the Norland College for over 20 years and was its principal for six.

Norland's students study for the Diploma in Childcare and Education or a BA (Hons) Early Childhood Studies in addition to the coveted Norland Diploma. The college arranges training placements in private homes in and around Bath and receives feedback from parents about how their students have worked. The college uses this feedback to help improve the students' standard of work during the remainder of their training. The college awards the world-renowned Norland Diploma to students who have completed the two-year training successfully and who have also worked competently for one year in probationary employment. A report to the college is made by the employer before the Norland Diploma can be awarded.

The Norland College has an agency situated on the college campus, which places its own graduates and provides excellent support to employers. This can be particularly useful for parents employing a nanny for the first time or when parents are grappling with the delights of newborn twins and wondering if they will ever enjoy an unbroken night's sleep in the forthcoming year! All Norland graduates remain accountable to the college, particularly during their probationary year and, therefore, employers know that both the college and the nanny have some responsibility for standards of work and practice.

The Chiltern Certificate

Chiltern College, situated in Caversham, Berkshire, is another private college. It opened in 1931 and prepares students to work in day nurseries, or as a nursery nurse in a school or with health visitors or holiday companies. The college's students also undertake the CACHE Diploma in Child Care and Education and some of its graduates choose to work as nannies while others work in the college's own nurseries. The college awards the Chiltern Certificate, which is a Level 3 qualification. The Chiltern College also assists its graduates to find appropriate employment.

PROFESSIONAL SKILLS

Studying for a childcare qualification enables the learner to gain those professional skills that are highly prized by employers. In addition to the personal skills previously identified, most employers are seeking someone with sound professional skills.

A childcare worker who has just gained a Level 3 qualification should be able to demonstrate all of the above professional skills but may not have had the experience to fit seamlessly into the role of a nanny in the private family. Newly qualified practitioners will need firm guidance as to the ways in which their employers wish

THE PERFECT NANNY'S PROFESSIONAL SKILLS

- Demonstrating principles of inclusion and equality of opportunity
- Respecting the principles of confidentiality
- Respecting the individual needs of each child
- Providing a safe environment for children
- Demonstrating a consistent approach to the children

- Working in partnership with and respecting the wishes of the parents
- Having a good understanding of child development
- Understanding the need for accountability
- Showing integrity and initiative
- Demonstrating effective childcare skills

the role to be carried out. It is far better for parents to provide this guidance from the beginning and to give feedback as to the success or otherwise of the nanny's efforts, rather than to be vague and then to complain that the job is not being carried out in a satisfactory manner.

THE NANNY SEARCH

Knowing something of early years qualifications enables parents to know in which direction they are heading with regard to the likely knowledge and skills of their ideal nanny. Is there such a person as the 'perfect nanny'? Well, perfection is subjective, but certainly there are many well-qualified and competent childcare workers who, when they understand the particular challenges of having the home as their workplace and are given some initial support, provide excellent childcare over a long period of time. Parents may find an ideal candidate who has years of childcare experience gained in a group setting but no experience as a nanny. Do not disregard this person, as most skilled, competent and professional carers will be able to make the transition from group care to the individual care of children. The challenge is for parents to match the skills, knowledge and experiences of their potential nanny to the needs of their family and children.

There are various ways of searching for a nanny. Years ago, many parents advertised in *The Lady* or the professional magazine *Nursery World*, but now a search can be carried out online. Look for further information in the 'Useful Sources' section at the back of the book. Sometimes a nanny can be found through the personal recommendation of a family whose children have 'outgrown' their nanny. It is not considered a good idea to 'poach' another family's dissatisfied nanny and entice them to your own household as this is unlikely to form the basis of a good professional relationship and can also be the end of a good friendship with the family who are now without a nanny.

USING A NANNY AGENCY

The majority of parents will approach a nanny agency to help them with their search. Check with each agency to find out what its charges cover. Fees should only be payable when a successful placement has been made. Fees may be charged at a percentage of the net annual salary, but will be different for a temporary, permanent, daily or resident nanny. Read the terms and conditions to see what happens in the event that the nanny leaves shortly after taking up his or her appointment: are the fees refunded in full, partly or not at all? An agency might charge a fee if a firm commitment has been made to employ a nanny and the employers then change their mind.

Before approaching an agency, make sure that you have made the decision as to what type of nanny you require. There are many nanny agencies that will help with this matching exercise. Agency staff will carry out many of the tasks connected with recruiting a nanny, but this does not mean that you cannot or should not be fully involved in the search process. The choice of nanny agency can be influenced by word of mouth, those available locally or those having membership of an organisation such as the Recruitment and

Employment Confederation (REC). Going to an agency affiliated to the REC means that an employer can look at its code of practice and have some reassurance that the recruitment practices are thorough. If choosing an agency, look for one that meets the REC Code of Practice. As always, parents are advised to check to make sure that the agency has carried out its responsibilities appropriately. Generally speaking, a code of practice means that a recommended agency will carry out certain duties with regard to the recruitment of a potential nanny.

AGENCY CODE OF PRACTICE – AN EXAMPLE OF WHAT TO LOOK FOR IN YOUR CHOSEN AGENCY

- All potential childcare workers are required to complete an application form giving personal information, qualifications, experience, employment and medical history
- Agency staff check original documentation
- Any gaps in employment history are explored and reasons requested for the gaps
- Each nanny's identity and approval to work in this country are checked

- The agency carries out an enhanced Criminal Records Bureau check
- All applicants are personally interviewed and their understanding of childcare issues explored
- A minimum of two references is taken up, including that of the most recent employer or training organisation; contact is made with the referees to confirm that the details included in the reference are correct

It is helpful to be aware that references are confidential between an employer and potential employer, whereas testimonials are not confidential and are written for anyone to read. In a confidential reference there may be a more honest and realistic appraisal of someone's work. A testimonial can be a more general summing-up of the person's good points and omit areas in need of development. Parents must decide which type of reference would satisfy them.

Reputable agencies also say that they will only put forward suitable candidates for consideration to a particular family and that full information will be given to both potential employee and employer before the actual interview.

It may be helpful to contact the early years tutors working in the local college of further education as often they will advertise nanny vacancies on their departmental notice board and may guide parents in the direction of some of their competent college leavers. However, there is unlikely to be any responsibility for the quality of work of a practitioner trained by the college.

WRITING THE JOB DESCRIPTION

When the nanny agency has been chosen, close collaboration is needed between parents and agency staff to ensure that the post to be filled is properly described in ways that are truthful, realistic and attractive to potential applicants. If a job description has been discussed and then written down all parties are clear as to the expectations of the parents. This will form the basis for discussion at interview and for the contract drawn up before the start of employment. The discipline of actually writing the job description means that points are clarified, but this does not mean that it is written in stone. As the process continues there are probably going to be second thoughts that may turn out to be better than the first. The more accurate the job description, the better prepared the nanny can be for the interview.

A job description is usually available to prospective nannies before the interview stage. When it has sufficient detail to give a realistic overview of the post available, a nanny considering applying can make an informed decision as to whether it would suit his or her particular qualifications, experiences and interests and/or provide a good opportunity to widen existing experience.

The agency staff should support parents in writing a job description. This will help them match the interests and skills of the nanny with his or her potential employer. Make sure that the job description gives a flavour of what working in your family and with your children will be like. A comprehensive job description facilitates good communication at the interview and in subsequent employment.

When the working relationship works well the job description will be rarely referred to, but when there is some disagreement it will be the first thing, together with the contract, that both parties reach for. Any changes to the job description that occur over time must be thoroughly discussed and mutually agreed. For example, one reason for a change would be that as children get older the duties of the nanny naturally change.

True life stories: If the cap fits...

Rebecca had completed two years working as a nanny and she had decided that she wanted to move on to another family in order to gain additional experience. She went for a preliminary interview with an agency and asked for details of jobs where the family was looking to employ a nanny for two children, one of whom would be a newborn. She left the agency offices with nine job descriptions and felt slightly daunted by the range of jobs on offer. Some of the job descriptions were very sketchy and she felt that she did not really have a good idea of what the family might be like. She was more interested in the posts where there was information about the children's activities and the family's general interests. She made a shortlist of the jobs where she had detailed information about the families and their lifestyles. From the details provided, she thought that she would fit into one of those families in particular.

The preferred job description had some information about the ways in which the mother described how she intended to care for her baby. It mentioned that the mother wanted to breastfeed her baby and that she would get up for the night feeds but would appreciate having an afternoon sleep when possible. This family also had a six-year-old son who was learning to swim. Rebecca had a swimming teacher's qualification and thought she would enjoy using her expertise with this family. Rebecca thought that the information gained from the job description would mean that she could prepare well for the interview and she asked the agency to arrange an interview for her.

SPECIAL REQUIREMENTS

If the family has specific religious or cultural requirements that will affect the nanny, such as the children not eating particular foods or requiring food to be prepared in a particular manner, it is important to state these requirements at the start of the recruitment process. Similarly, inform prospective nannies if you own any pets or animals as they may be allergic to certain animals and would find themselves unable to accept such a post. If any of the children has a particular talent or disability that the nanny needs to be aware of make sure that it is referred to in the job description.

A typical job description looks like this:

Job description for nanny for Caroline aged three-and-a-half and Elizabeth aged seven months. Family lives in Bristol. Small garden. No pets.

☐ Resident nanny is on duty from 7am to children's bedtime, usually 7pm

☐ Nanny is required to babysit two or three times a week

☐ Two consecutive days off each week

☐ Prepare all Caroline's meals each week for a seven-day period using only organic ingredients

☐ Prepare daily all formula feeds for Elizabeth. Prepare and freeze weaning foods

☐ Wash and dress both children, brush hair, clean teeth, etc.

☐ Feed Caroline and Elizabeth breakfast, lunch and tea together with drinks

☐ Clean and tidy the kitchen and dining area after each meal. Mop the floor daily

☐ Fill and empty the dishwasher daily

☐ Do the children's laundry. Dry and iron clothes. Put clothes away in children's bedrooms

☐ On pre-schools days, take/collect Caroline to/from pre-school. Do not leave Elizabeth in the car!

☐ Ensure Elizabeth has morning and afternoon sleep

☐ Dust, vacuum and tidy the children's bedrooms and ensure toys and books are well looked after

☐ Take children to doctor/health visitor/baby clinic/dentist when required

☐ Organise appropriate activities to benefit the children

☐ On a daily basis spend at least one hour, hopefully longer, enjoying stories, songs and action rhymes with both children

☐ Keep a written account of monies spent on food and children's clothes shopping

☐ Keep a daily diary of meals, activities, special events (such as first words, first steps, etc.)

☐ Communicate any emergency situation immediately to parents using mobile phone

CHAPTER 3

HOW TO INTERVIEW AND SELECT THE PERFECT NANNY

In this chapter, parents will find out about the various aspects connected with interviewing potential candidates for their nanny position. As with all interviewing procedures, there is no guaranteed method to ensure the perfect candidate can be easily and quickly identified, but there are ways in which some pitfalls can be avoided. Previous chapters have identified the need for a job description and a contract and it is during the interview process that these documents can be so helpful. At this point they form the basis for the interview. The content can be amended slightly after discussion, but parents need to be clear in their minds about what is negotiable and what is not. Do not negotiate on matters you consider extremely important as this is likely to cause anxiety in the future.

This chapter will cover aspects of the interview process including:

- *Preparing for the interview*
- *The first interview*
- *The second interview*
- *Making the decision*

PREPARING FOR THE INTERVIEW

It is not only the potential nanny who has to prepare for the interview, it is also the employer! Time spent preparing to interview the candidates is well spent. However, before the actual interview takes place there are more decisions to make.

If possible, have several candidates to interview, all of whom should match the 'person specification' of your perfect nanny. Although this will vary from family to family, top of the list must be someone who likes and enjoys the company of young children and, secondly, someone who shares the approach and philosophy of childcare held by you, the parents. The person specification should list the aspects that must be found in your perfect nanny and identify those aspects that are non-negotiable.

ESSENTIAL AREAS FOR AN EMPLOYER TO CONSIDER BEFOREHAND AND BE PREPARED TO DISCUSS AT INTERVIEW

- Starting date
- Accommodation that can be provided for the nanny, if a resident post
- Salary – make clear whether it is a gross or net amount
- Holiday entitlement and when this can be taken
- The time the nanny will be 'off duty' – is it always at the weekend?

- Household duties that the nanny will be expected to complete
- Particular requirements of the employer, such as setting the alarm when leaving the house, or not having friends over during 'working hours'
- Any benefits, such as use of a car, private health scheme or membership of a gym

An Example of a Person Specification

Mr and Mrs G would like to employ a nanny who is totally trustworthy and has at least two years' childcare experience, preferably as a nanny. Our ideal nanny will be someone who enjoys the company of our two lively daughters, aged four and one, and will be able to encourage them in their development. The children enjoy outdoor life and our nanny should be fond of walks in the countryside, visiting the park and zoo and swimming trips. Our nanny should be a competent, imaginative cook who can make a variety of meals from fresh ingredients. We have separate accommodation for our nanny and the use of a nanny car.

Remember that it is considered 'good practice' to offer interview expenses to all applicants.

PRE-INTERVIEW CHECKS

It is important to ensure that the agency has your (the employer's) details correct and describes the job accurately, but also attractively. Make clear to the agency staff that you only wish to interview people who fit your person specification. If you have decided not to use an agency it is even more important to stick to your original thoughts and to remember the reasons why you drew up the person specification. This will help you to be more efficient when deciding who to interview.

SCRUTINISING THE NANNY CV

If agency staff are involved in the recruitment process, prior to the interviews they should have met the candidates, carried out the basic checks and provided some feedback for employers. They should also have given parents the candidates' CVs, which need to be read carefully before interviewing. Remember, if the agency has a common format for the nanny CV, it may not tell parents as much about the candidate as a CV prepared solely by the nanny.

Look for basic information in the CV, such as qualifications and experience, but also look for information about children previously cared for and knowledge and skills related to the position being applied for, such as the ability to look after children who require special diets. Also look for interests that are shared by the nanny and the family, such as swimming, horse riding or artistic and creative skills perhaps. For older children, the nanny's interests can often be the start of some hobbies and sporting interests for them.

Check for any gaps in employment history and be sure to discuss this during the interview. It is perfectly acceptable to have some time away from work travelling, but during any discussion it should be apparent that this actually took place and hopefully some benefit gained. Alarm bells should ring if there is any hesitant or unsatisfactory explanation of the time not covered in the CV.

Search the CV for evidence that the nanny is committed to a career in childcare. For example, have additional post-basic qualifications been achieved or particular professional interests followed up, such as training in the care of babies or weaning? And, to avoid wasting everybody's time, make a last check of the CV to be certain that there are no aspects that will definitely rule out a particular candidate, such as an allergy to cats where the employer is a committed cat lover.

Hopefully, there will be at least five suitable candidates to interview, but the employer needs to have a system to remember each of the candidates. One way of doing this is to have a checklist (see below) to be completed once after reading each CV and then again after each interview.

45

INTERVIEW NOTES

An interview checklist will ensure that all the important ground is covered and that a fair comparison can be made between each of the candidates. It is also advisable to include in the list items that form the employers' ground rules. In this way an employer will be certain that these points have been discussed during the interview and that any candidate who finds them unacceptable does not end up on the shortlist. Use the checklist as the basis for the interview and make notes on the candidates' responses to each of the points.

KEY CHECKLIST POINTS

- Reasons for applying for this particular post
- Qualifications
- Experience with children of what age and number of children looked after at any one time
- Particular experience required, such as working with twins or triplets
- Special skills required, such as working with a child who has autism

- Evidence of additional training undertaken by the nanny
- Experience of and willingness to travel as part of the job
- Driving licence and years of experience driving with any accidents noted
- Willingness to accept a contract of a particular period
- 'Ground rules' fully discussed

Remember to adapt the checklist to your own requirements and to definitely include those aspects that you regard as non-negotiable.

EMPLOYER GROUND RULES

When ground rules are clearly stated at the outset, they will be seen as the views of an employer who has firm guidelines rather than as personally aimed at any one particular nanny. Possible ground rules may include:

- Be clear as to what you consider appropriate dress to be worn 'on duty', e.g. are you happy for your nanny to wear jeans or skimpy tops?
- Be clear about your views on boyfriends or girlfriends staying overnight: what is your view about those in a long-term, stable relationship that you may get to know in time?
- State clearly that on no occasion are the children to be smacked but also be clear about your approach to the positive management of the children's behaviour and the ways in which

both nanny and parent should adopt a consistent approach for the children's benefit.

- Are you prepared for your nanny to join a nanny circle for daily socialising when your baby is only a few months old or do you think that this is not in the best interest of your baby? Be aware that very young babies benefit from a regular routine with lots of sleep and do not need to socialise with a great many people outside of the home environment.

- Do you wish your resident nanny to be home before a certain time prior to each working day or are you relaxed about this as long as the job is professionally carried out and your children are properly cared for?

- If you wish the children's clothes to be colour coordinated or immaculately folded when they are put away after laundering be certain to discuss this at interview.

- Do you want to restrict the number of hours your children spend watching television or list appropriate programmes that can be watched with the nanny?

- Decide if you are going to insist that there is no smoking in your home or at any time with the children and whether any alcohol can be consumed while 'on duty'. Make clear your viewpoint on the zero-tolerance of non-medicinal drugs. Clarify what any nanny might mean by being a 'social smoker'.

- Be adamant about the importance to you of confidentiality both while in your employment and forever after.

- If you wish all the children's food to be home-prepared with organic ingredients make this very clear.

- Are you going to restrict the use of the car to nanny duties? Be clear about what the employer will pay for with regard to fuel, insurance, car tax and maintenance. Also be clear that the nanny is responsible for parking tickets and any speeding fines. Check how regularly the nanny has driven since passing her driving test, as it is preferable that driving experience is gained at a time when not responsible for your children. If previous experience has been within a quiet rural area and the post is in a busy city

47

environment, arrange for some additional lessons to be had and time given to gain driving experience in the local area.

- Be clear about what you regard as legitimate use of the nanny phone. Will you have a mobile 'nursery duties only' phone with an itemised monthly bill? If so, be clear that you will check the bill for any anomalies and then discus these, if necessary.
- If employing a resident nanny, do you wish to ensure your privacy in the evenings and weekends? Some employers wish the nanny to go away for the weekends and to have some parts of their house out of bounds in the evenings. However, think what this means for the nanny. Does she need to be bright and sociable by day and a recluse by night? Where will she go at weekends?

It is possible to include some of the really important 'ground rules' in the contract and to identify those which, if broken, are grounds for instant dismissal, such as neglect of the children or putting their safety at risk, together with any single instance of stealing, lying, drug or alcohol abuse. It is much better to start off with a really firm regime and then to consider any relaxations when integrity has been demonstrated and a trusting relationship has been achieved through professional hard work and competency.

A nanny will expect each employer to have a set of ground rules and if they are presented in a friendly manner will not be put off by a full list but will welcome the guidance. Make sure as far as possible that there are no surprises for the nanny or the employer after the job has started.

WHERE TO INTERVIEW

The best place to interview is in the place of work, i.e. the employer's home, as it gives the candidates the opportunity to see where they might be working. However, this can pose the employer with a dilemma. If the home is a scene of happy turmoil strewn with children's toys mingled with the tools of an artist's trade and the occasional empty coffee cup, should the house be tidied, vacuumed and dusted beforehand? This might create a good impression, but is it a good idea to give a false impression? Honesty is the best policy, and the nanny might feel that this is a very suitable and relaxed home. If, however, it appears to the nanny to be a home where a chaotic situation might prevent a good job from being done it is best for him or her to realise this at interview stage rather than after the job has been accepted. Or, if your house offers a welcoming home to two frisky Dalmatians, for example, it is best that the nanny meets them at the interview stage and decides whether they will be a fun part of the job or a hindrance, rather than meeting the dogs for the first time on day one of the employment.

WHO SHOULD INTERVIEW?

Regardless of any interviewing work carried out by agency staff, it is essential that parents are fully involved in the interview process. It is always better for two people to carry out the interview as then a proper discussion about each candidate can be had. Possibly, one person can make a few notes while the other asks the questions. Try to make the interview a three-way discussion rather then an intimidating interrogation, as in this way you will enable each candidate to show the best of themselves and to ask the questions that are important to them. Remember, the interview is a two-way process: parents may need to persuade an excellent applicant that their job is the one to accept!

THE FIRST INTERVIEW

It is important not to carry out too many interviews at any one time as exhaustion can set in, and when it does there may not be fair treatment for all candidates. If interviewing five or six candidates then two interview sessions are recommended. Allow plenty of time for each person: for the candidate to look round the home and the accommodation, if resident, and to meet the children, if possible; for the interview itself and any questions from the candidate; for a discussion after the candidate has left; and to complete the checklist. For the first interview, it is not essential for very young children to be present as parents then can fully concentrate on each applicant. If the children are asleep or at pre-school be certain to arrange the second interview so that the nanny and the children can meet.

It is very helpful to the candidate if he or she is told the likely format of the interview and reassured that there will be plenty of time for his or her questions. If two people are interviewing, decide beforehand who will ask which questions and allow each interviewer to follow through on answers requiring further probing – this allows the candidate to think through his or her answer rather than having to field different questions from two people.

Begin with basic questions that are centred on the job description. Make the first few questions the sort that the candidate will be expecting. In this way you are putting him or her at ease but also starting the interviewing process in a business-like and professional manner. These initial questions will focus on qualifications and the knowledge and experience gained at this time, and will be followed by further questions about his or her previous experience with children. If the candidate has only recently gained his or her qualification, questions can still be asked about childcare experiences as he or she should be able to refer to placements undertaken during training. Some candidates may have had only group childcare experience, perhaps in a day nursery, and are looking for a career change in a related field. If so, be sure to ask questions about how they would plan for the individual needs of the children and how they would ensure that a variety of experiences both inside and outside the home would be planned.

Ask questions related to the age of your children with regard to their stage of development and the stages of development that will soon follow. Expect the candidate to be knowledgeable about child development and what children of a certain age are likely to be able to do, as knowing about child development is the key to working professionally with children.

Questions also need to be asked that reflect possible situations that may occur in your family life. Such questions will be different for every family but may include:

- We are hoping to have another baby in the next few months. How would you suggest that we help our son Jack to cope with all the changes?
- My mother-in-law is going to move into the granny annex next month. How will you ensure that the twins can enjoy her company but do not get spoilt by her?
- I intend to work from home more. How do you suggest that we explain to Sophie that although I will be at home, it will be her nanny who is looking after her?

Some interviewers will ask questions about the long-term plans of the nanny, but in reality this is 'crystal ball' gazing and should not unduly influence any decisions that may be made.

After your pre-planned questions have been asked, remember to ask questions that relate to the candidate's CV, any employment gaps that need to be explored or any issues raised by interesting aspects of previous experiences. Check that you have given all of the required information about the post, including your ground rules. Be prepared to discuss your ground rules but remember which aspects of the job you have agreed are non-negotiable.

SOME USEFUL INTERVIEW QUESTIONS

- **'Tell me how you would plan the day for my two children, aged nine months and three years, when, due to the baby feeling unwell, it is not possible to take the children out?'**

Listen for an answer that includes plenty of play, stories and fun creative activities for the three-year-old and some quiet times with cuddles and rest for the baby. Games in the garden for the older child, so as not to disturb the baby while he or she sleeps, would be a good idea.

continued on next page

51

• 'What sort of activities outside the home would you plan for my two children?'

In this answer, the potential nanny should show an awareness of putting the children's needs first; visits to the library, swimming pool and park are preferable to an endless round of busy nanny network circles.

• 'I want my children to have all home-prepared and -cooked meals. What would be your menu plan for the week?'

Variety and a willingness to make meals attractive and appealing to children are the watchwords here. Ask for more than two days' menus as this will help to show competence. Not all nanny training covers the basics of menu planning, so this is an aspect to investigate in some depth. Check to see that the applicant understands the various food groups and the way in which meals are properly balanced. If appropriate, listen for ideas in which the children can be involved in food preparation. Do not be satisfied if all meals consist of pasta and a variety of sauces. Also question how food preparation and cooking will be combined with other nursery duties.

• 'My nine-month-old baby shows few signs of wanting to communicate verbally. What would you do in this situation?'

Listen for a response that shows understanding of the fact that all children develop in different ways and that one child who seems slower than others in talking may also be the same child who is walking and running much earlier than any of his or her contemporaries. A reassuring note should be balanced by emphasis on the need for many stories, much conversation and a vast repertoire of songs, poems and fun action rhymes.

• 'My job requires long working hours and sometimes I have to stay late at short notice. Although you would normally go off duty at 6.30 pm, occasionally I would need you to stay to carry out bathtime and bedtime routine. What would you do in these circumstances?'

Look for a response that indicates a willingness to help out in any emergency situation. Accept as reasonable a nanny's request for as much notice as possible so that his or her own arrangements can be taken care of.

• 'What current first-aid qualifications do you have and how would you deal with a medical emergency?'

Hopefully, the nanny will be in possession of a current paediatric first-aid certificate, and will tell you that – after dealing with the emergency to the best of his or her abilities, contacting the appropriate professional, and reassuring any other children – he or she would immediately contact the parents, fully inform them of the situation and agree with them the next course of action.

It is often helpful to provide a real-life scenario, such as your child falling and cutting his or her knee on a sharp stone.

• 'If my three-year-old's pre-school phones to say that there has been an accident and that it is advisable for my child to go to the hospital accident and emergency department, what would you do?'

In this event, expect the nanny to say that the parents would be contacted immediately and a discussion would be had as to who would go to hospital and who would be responsible for any other children. Have a follow-up question ready to see what the nanny would do if the parents were briefly unavailable.

continued on next page

- 'My three-year-old asks you if he can watch "CBeebies" every afternoon. As we have discussed, you know that I allow some television watching occasionally but certainly not on a daily basis. Matthew tells you that Mummy allows him to do this every day. You explain that this is not the case and Matthew has a tantrum. Do you allow him to watch the television?'

Listen for a response that shows that the nanny adopts a consistent approach in tune with your guidelines. The nanny should say that Matthew will be told that this has been discussed with his mother and that this is the joint decision. However, there should also be an understanding of the child's interests and that regular time will be spent with Matthew on activities connected with the television programme, perhaps using a children's magazine that has some of the television characters as its focus.

INTERVIEWEE RESPONSES

Be alert to the candidates' responses to your questions, not only to the content of their answers but also to the way in which they answer. Childcare practitioners who enjoy their work also revel in talking about their experiences with children and usually reflect their delight through the warmth of their answers and the way in which they expand their responses with examples of their various experiences with families or in placements. Reflect on how they speak about families they have worked for previously, as although it may not have been a consistently harmonious relationship it should always be discussed and referred to in a professional and courteous manner. Listen for any breaches of confidentiality and where this takes place think about the way in which your own family matters may be discussed by this candidate in the future. In this situation, the candidate may not be the nanny for your family as you could not be certain that family matters would remain within the family. It is essential that you feel confident that family finances, business and personal relationships remain within the home.

Remember that the candidates will have had your job description and information about your family and should be prepared for specific questions if they have carried out their interview preparation thoroughly. If they cannot answer these very relevant questions satisfactorily ask yourself if they are serious about the position.

QUESTIONS FROM THE CANDIDATE

Ask the candidate for any questions. Do not be dismayed if he or she takes a long list out of his or her pocket, as this shows that the interviewee has planned for the interview and has thought seriously about the post and the ways in which he or she might carry out the role. At this point in the interview all parties should feel sufficiently comfortable to ask all the questions that need to be asked and to have every opportunity to discuss all aspects of the job.

True life stories: Tom's queries

Tom always felt nervous about interviews, especially the part where employers asked whether he had any questions. Nevertheless, he generally did well at interviews and had always been offered the posts that he had interviewed for, although he did not always accept them. One way of dealing with his nerves was to write down the questions he wanted to ask. He had started doing this after his very first interview for a nanny post when he realised that he had finished the interview, left the employer's home and then realised that many of his queries were unanswered. He felt annoyed with himself and resolved not to let this happen again.

His questions for Mr and Mrs T were about the children's routines, their views on discipline, the hours they worked and the particular qualities and experiences they looked for in a nanny. He was surprised by the long hours they said they worked and realised that this would mean an extended working day for him. They did, however, say that occasionally he would be able to leave early on a Friday afternoon. The long hours concerned him and he was pleased that he had clarified this point. He liked the way in which the children seemed to have stability in their daily routines but he decided that he would have to take some time to think about whether this job was right for him.

After the interview Mrs T was impressed with the way he had prepared. She thought that it was a good indication of the way in which he approached his work and she would be pleased if he accepted their job.

BRINGING THE INTERVIEW TO AN END

When each first interview has finished, remember to tell the candidate what will happen next. Inform them that you will be making a shortlist and inviting some candidates back for a second interview and that these interviews will take place on the date stated on the job description. Thank the candidate for attending the interview and make sure that interview expenses have been settled.

When all of the first-round interviews have been completed, read the notes taken during interviews together with the notes made immediately afterwards. Complete any gaps in the interview checklist and then reflect on what has been written down. Think about whether your interview notes give a realistic impression of the person you met.

True life stories: First impressions

Emma and Dan met Kizzie for the first time when they interviewed her for their nanny post. Prior to the interview they had formed an impression that she was very well organised as her CV was well presented and detailed. She had phoned beforehand to check on the travel details and she also asked if she would be able to meet the children when she came for the interview. Emma was optimistic that they might have found the right person for their family. When Kizzie arrived for her interview, Emma's first impressions were confirmed. She was punctual and well prepared for her interview. With the agreement of her previous employers, she had brought with her some photos of her work and Dan could see that she really enjoyed being with children and planning many artistic activities for them. From the photos, it could also be seen that she frequently took the children out to the park, into the garden and to the library. Kizzie spoke warmly of her other jobs and still kept in contact with the children. She seemed genuinely interested in their progress and maintained a professional approach. Emma and Dan decided that they might like to have Kizzie as their nanny and decided to invite her back for a second interview. They made a note of the points that they wanted further detail on and looked forward to finding out more about her.

POST INTERVIEW REFLECTION

- Which candidates most closely match the requirements of the post as outlined in the job description?
- Which candidates most closely match your person specification?
- Which candidates would you like to look after your children and to have around your home?
- Who could you trust to be totally reliable and provide a safe and happy environment for your children?

SHORTLISTING

Allow sufficient time between first and second interviews for a shortlist to be drawn up, discussion to take place with agency staff (if used) and for references to be taken up on those candidates invited back for a second interview. References are essential and provide another insight into the candidates' experience, but read them with an open mind and be prepared to form your own opinion and to make your own judgement.

Ideally you are looking for two candidates to shortlist. However, it is often helpful to have a third person identified who would be a possible candidate for the second round. This is because one of your ideal applicants may have decided that your family is not for them! It is also possible that another post has already been accepted.

When an agreement has been reached as to whom you will invite back, let all of the candidates know what their position is. An agency will wish to have some feedback about the candidates that it put forward. It is also likely that all unsuccessful candidates would appreciate information about why they have not been selected for a second interview. If this is the case, give some positive feedback together with ways in which they did not fully meet the requirements of the job description; this may help them to be successful in future applications. Only a brief response is required, and the notes made for the checklist should help.

If, at this point, there are absolutely no candidates that you could envisage looking after your children, it is better to admit this and to go back to stage one, perhaps rewriting your advert if returning to the original agency, or selecting another agency.

Now, hopefully, there are two worthwhile candidates left. However, preparations need to be made for their second interviews.

THE SECOND INTERVIEW

The second interview should last at least one day (with the children present) and resemble a typical working day for the nanny, albeit with the employer present. For a resident nanny, the second interview should include an overnight stay.

ORGANISING THE DAY

The organisation for the second interview day is important. Make sure that the candidate knows how the day will be structured. For a resident post this second interview will also include helping with bathtime and bedtime routines for the children and an overnight stay. This enables all parties to understand how the other functions first thing in the morning, which can be a frantic time in family life when everybody is not at their best!

WHY HOLD A SECOND INTERVIEW?

The reason for the second interview is to help parents get to know their potential nanny better and also:

- to confirm the impressions gained at first interview
- to check any small queries brought to light in the first interview
- to confirm information on the reference or at least to reconcile any perceived differences

- to have more time to get to know the nanny's personality and characteristics
- to observe professional competency
- to observe the interaction between nanny and children
- to ask the children their views, where possible
- to decide if you would enjoy the nanny's company (especially important for a resident post)
- to make the final decision

Make sure that any resident nanny accommodation is how it will be if an appointment is made or, if not, explain carefully why this is the case. If the accommodation is not ready, it is important to clarify what the arrangements will be in the first few weeks of employment and then what any final arrangements might be. However, this is not a favourable situation as it brings more uncertainties into an already 'precarious' situation for the nanny who may well be on the verge of giving notice on a perfectly satisfactory job to gain new experience.

It is very helpful for the parent who will be 'overseeing' the day to write down an outline of the daily routine, indicating mealtimes and other fixed events, such as when one of the children is due home from pre-school. In this way the relationship will get off to a good start, the nanny can be a little more comfortable in the new situation, the children can keep to their usual routine and everybody will have more time to get to know each other. Leave plenty of time for play, songs and stories and other creative activities or a visit to the park. In this way the children will be able to interact and enjoy the company of their new nanny and there will also be plenty of time for observation.

It is not a good idea to give too much responsibility to the candidate during the second interview day. The parents should still collect their child from pre-school and cook the meals, but hopefully ably and willingly assisted by the nanny.

On some occasions the potential nanny will work alongside the current nanny. Although possibly a tricky situation for all, remember that consistency and continuity for the children are paramount. If the children are old enough, explain to them what is happening but expect some changes in their behaviour, especially if their present nanny has been with them for a long time, perhaps since they were born. All professional and competent nannies will understand the reasons for this and should be more than capable of managing the situation.

It is perfectly acceptable for the new nanny to want to discuss the post with the current nanny. Where the relationship has been happy and successful this is a good thing as the new nanny will have any positive thoughts about the job confirmed and small queries resolved. The current nanny will also be able to add her opinion about the new nanny and, where there has been a mutually trusting and respectful working relationship, this will add another helpful perspective to the impending decision. Where the relationship between nanny and parent has been a little fraught, a decision will have to be made about whether to depend on the professional approach of the current nanny or whether to give her the day off.

When the end of the working day has finished, it is advisable to give each of the applicants the time and opportunity to have any of their remaining questions answered and also for the parents to resolve any outstanding queries. For a resident appointment, this can be achieved over supper, but do not make this too long an event as both parties will be feeling rather tired.

Remember to thank the nanny for his or her time and assistance and give the candidate some idea as to when you will be making your final decision. It is as well to let the person know if there is another second interview still to take place but remember that he or she may also be attending other interviews and may have a decision to make over whether to accept the job. It is still a two-way process!

A final point: remember to pay the interview expenses.

Once the candidate has left, make some additional notes to add to the first interview notes. If appropriate, listen to the opinions of the children and the current nanny. Depending on the age of the children, listen to their views but remember that they may be sad about losing their current nanny and may not be keen on any changes. Make your decision based on who you think is the better candidate, not solely on your children's preference.

Although the agency will want some feedback, it is important that you have the time to make some considered judgements, so do not be rushed at this point.

MAKING THE DECISION

If it is entirely obvious as to who should be appointed, the decision-making could be a short process. Far harder is the situation in which each of the candidates has several outstanding features and both candidates can be regarded as having equal merit. In which case a plan of action is necessary.

Re-read the job description and make certain that it really does reflect the job that you want done. Consider each of the applicants and note their capabilities against each element of the job description. Use your checklist and your additional notes to do this. Look again at the references. Now might be a good time to telephone each of the referees to discuss with them what has been written in the reference. Listen to the tone of voice, to any hesitations and to anything that may be left unsaid: this can be just as important as what is actually said. A good question could be, 'Would you employ this person again?', followed by 'Why?' or 'Why not?'.

THE FOLLOWING QUESTIONS COULD ALSO HELP YOU MAKE THE DECISION:

- What was your first impression of the candidate? Did this impression change during the course of the interview? If so, why?
- Did he or she smile, make eye contact and seem pleased to be at the interview?
- Had the candidate prepared well for the interview?
- Had he or she attended the first and second interviews appropriately dressed?
- Were nails short and clean and hair well cared for?
- Was the candidate punctual? If not, what was the reason?
- How did he or she show professionalism?
- Did he or she carry out tasks competently at the second interview?

- Through conversation and actions, was a knowledge and understanding shown of how children develop?
- How did the candidate show interest in your job and in your children?
- Did he or she play with the children?
- Was he or she able to chat happily with the children and to follow their lead?
- Was the candidate able to 'tune into' the children?
- Were there plenty of songs, stories and action rhymes?
- Did he or she support you with a united front when managing the children?
- Did you like the candidate and want to spend time with that person and help him or her settle into your job?

If the answer to all of the above questions is 'Yes' you may have found your perfect nanny. If the answers are mostly 'Yes' you still may have found your perfect nanny but must be prepared to invest time and energy to achieve perfection. If the answer to only a few of these questions is 'Yes' think carefully before making the appointment.

Make a final check that qualifications and experience have been confirmed and that the CRB check is complete and up to date.

Assuming that you now have found your perfect nanny, telephone the successful candidate, say how delighted you are with the situation in offering the post and confirm the starting date and the salary. Say that you will prepare two copies of the contract and will soon be in touch to explain how the settling-in period will be managed. Now contact the agency, pay its fees and provide some feedback on its service. Remember also to contact the unsuccessful candidates and to thank them for their interest. It is best to do this only once your chosen nanny has accepted the post in case your first choice does not accept your offer.

TELLING THE CHILDREN

Once your nanny has accepted your offer of employment and you have taken care of arrangements with the agency, there is one further important task to be completed: telling your children.

Think about how you will prepare the children and what reasons you will give for the forthcoming change. Being truthful about the need for a parent to return to work is always easiest, using language that the children will understand. Be ready to answer their questions about why you will not be at home during the day and also about the new nanny.

Expect that the children may be upset and disgruntled. It may take some time for the children to get used to the changes but if everyone remains positive then children usually adapt quite quickly.

CHAPTER 4

EMPLOYER RESPONSIBILITIES

Having offered a job to a nanny, parents take on the responsibilities of an employer, perhaps finding themselves in this surprisingly complex situation for the first time. Many parents decide to use a specialist payroll company to pay the nanny and help take care of some of these responsibilities, and if you used a supportive recruitment agency to find your new nanny, then its staff will also be able to guide you though your various duties as an employer. Nevertheless, parents need to understand what these responsibilities are so that they know everything is as it should be, and should ask to be kept fully informed and involved.

This chapter will help parents to be aware of their responsibilities when employing a nanny. It contains information on:

- *Carrying out checks on your nanny*
- *Tax, pay and holidays*
- *The contract of employment*

CARRYING OUT CHECKS ON YOUR NANNY

A very important check to make is the one connected with the enhanced Criminal Records Bureau (CRB). If the agency does this search, an employer must know when it was carried out, as the information is only as good as the day the check was made. There is no way of knowing what happened, if anything, after the date it took place. Make sure that the agency carries out a CRB check on all potential nannies on your short list. Look also at the date on a first-aid certificate to see if it is current. You should also look at qualification certificates; the awarding body the Council for Awards in Children's Care and Education (CACHE) offers a service for employers to check early years qualifications (*see* Useful Sources *on page 136*).

THE OFSTED CHILDCARE REGISTER

Ofsted childcare registration is not compulsory for home-based childcarers such as nannies. However, as mentioned in Chapter 1, this style of care can be registered on the voluntary part of the register and there are numerous benefits in doing this for both parent and nanny: a certificate of registration is provided that can be shown to parents who request it; the parent may be eligible to claim the childcare element of the working tax credit; and the nanny can demonstrate to a parent that he or she meets the Ofsted requirements with regard to people who have access to the children, the premises where childcare is provided and the standard of care provided.

Ofsted inspects a proportion of voluntarily registered provision and after doing so will provide a letter relating to its findings, which is published on its website (*see* Useful Sources *on page 136*). Nannies registered with Ofsted will have been required to have an enhanced CRB disclosure, an identity check, a current first-aid certificate and evidence as to their suitability to provide childcare. Parents can also check with Ofsted as to the currency of any registration.

65

THE CV

Applicants for a nanny post will have provided a CV, either compiled and written by the individual or put together in the corporate style of an agency. Parents need to remember that on any CV the contents are those decided by the individual or are those that he or she has perhaps been advised to include by an agency. It is unlike an application form where the employer decides on the content and the individual supplies answers to specific questions.

TAX, PAY AND HOLIDAYS
HM REVENUE AND CUSTOMS

The moment when a nanny begins work for a family, the parent becomes an employer and must comply with various pieces of legislation. The employer must register with HM Revenue and Customs (HMRC), which has an employer help line and provides a new employer's pack full of helpful information. Employer registration can be made online on its website.

There are companies such as PAYE for Nannies, Nanny Tax and Guardian Angels who will assist employers with managing the payment of salaries as well as making the appropriate deductions, such as tax and National Insurance, in addition to preparing monthly or weekly payslips and annual end-of-year financial summaries, including P60 summaries. The provision of payslips is a legal requirement. Payroll companies charge a small annual fee and offer advice and support to employers. In addition to these deductions made to HMRC on behalf of their nanny, employers must also pay the employer's National Insurance contribution based on the nanny's gross annual wage.

If a nanny is employed by two families then this is termed a 'nanny share' and HMRC may have different requirements for National Insurance and tax deductions; either HMRC or the selected payroll company will be able to advise. It may be that the best course of action is for each family to set up its own separate PAYE schemes as this may result in some savings for each family with regard to National Insurance payments without having any negative effect on the nanny. However, parents must check to ensure that they are complying with current legislation and take appropriate advice, and they would be well advised to use a payroll service so that they do not have the added worry of meeting employment legislation.

STATUTORY SICK PAY

Responsibilities also include the appropriate payment of Statutory Sick Pay (SSP). SSP is legally payable from the fourth working day off sick. Many employers decide to improve these conditions and pay the normal salary for a short period in any period of absence; however, parents may wish to state that these payments above the SSP will be limited to a specific number of weeks in any twelve-month period. Seek advice on the exact payment to be made and the terms of eligibility, as these can differ according to circumstances and the nanny's weekly wage. It is also a good idea to explain in the contract what you as an employer will do in these circumstances and also what actions you expect the employee to carry out. You may like to include a statement such as:

☐ The Employee shall be entitled to receive full pay for the first four weeks of sickness and then Statutory Sick Pay only, at the rate stipulated by the Government, for a further 24 weeks. Qualifying days for Statutory Sick Pay will be Monday to Friday.

☐ The Employee shall provide the Employer with medical evidence relating to any sickness or injury that has continued for three or more days by providing a sickness certificate showing the cause of sickness or injury, signed by a GP. Sickness certificates will have to be provided for the whole period of absence from work.

STATUTORY MATERNITY PAY

Other responsibilities extend to the payment of Statutory Maternity Pay (SMP) if the employee becomes pregnant while working for the employer and earns more than a certain amount each week. Currently, SMP is taxable and is paid at 90 per cent of the normal gross wage for the first six weeks of maternity leave and then at a flat rate of £112.75 for a further 33 weeks. In most cases the employer can reclaim all of the SMP from HMRC. A further period of unpaid leave may be taken: up to 12 months maternity leave in total. The nanny remains employed throughout this period and the employer is required to allow the employee to return to her job at the end of her maternity leave. Parents choosing to use a payroll service will be advised as to what their legal responsibilities are.

HOLIDAY ENTITLEMENT

An agreement between the nanny and employer regarding holidays should be made before the contract is drawn up. Employees who work on a full-time basis are entitled to four weeks' paid holiday each year. Some employers like to state when two of these four weeks should be taken and then negotiate with their nanny when the remaining two weeks will be taken. Usually, bank holidays are thought of as holidays in addition to the annual leave. Parents need to consider whether they will only agree to holidays being taken after the nanny has worked a sufficient period of time for the holiday entitlement to be accrued.

NANNY APPROVAL SCHEME

Childcare Vouchers are not means tested and are, therefore, available to most families. To obtain these vouchers, parents need to take part in a Childcare Vouchers scheme operated by the employer of a parent. If part of the nanny salary is to be paid by an employer through a Childcare Vouchers scheme, the nanny must be qualified and approved under the government approvals scheme. This approval is normally given when the nanny has a suitable childcare qualification at certificate level or above together with a valid first-aid qualification and an enhanced CRB check. The nanny should have an Approval Letter containing a unique approval number that is current. The cost of obtaining this Approval Letter is approximately £96 each year.

INSURANCE

By law, as an employer you are obliged to take out employers' liability insurance with regard to your nanny. This insurance will protect you against costs and compensation awards that could be made if you are held responsible for an injury sustained by your nanny in the course of carrying out duties in your home or while out and about. Check your household insurance to see if you already have such cover in place, and if it appears so, double-check to make certain that your employment of a nanny is covered. You will also need to ascertain that you have adequate motor insurance cover, as 'nanny use' may be considered to require business insurance. There are some specialist childcare insurers available to help you with these matters.

True life stories: A daunting task

Rob and Katy had decided to employ a daily nanny for their twins. They had busy professional lives and liked to socialise. The twins enjoyed going to their childminder but did not seem to spend much time in their own home, so some things, such as the children's clothes and toys, were becoming neglected. Katy decided that employing a nanny would be of help to the whole family. Once they started finding out what would be expected of them as employers, they were surprised at what was involved. However, by doing some reading and research, they found various companies who could help with all the legal issues and their employment responsibilities They contacted a nanny agency, who recommended one such company and were pleasantly surprised at how easy everything was and how knowledgeable and helpful the staff were. Rob decided to investigate with his employers the possibility of using childcare vouchers through the salary sacrifice scheme. They agreed to this and Rob decided to nominate the maximum amount he could, which was £55 per week. He completed the form agreeing to a lower 'cash' salary and was pleased with the financial saving he would make through the reduction in the amount of tax and National Insurance he would pay.

THE CONTRACT OF EMPLOYMENT

Employment law requires that every nanny must have a contract of employment within 28 days of starting work. Two copies of the contract are required to be signed and dated by both parties and one copy held by each party. A contract is drawn up based on the job description discussed at interview. It helps to clarify the nanny duties, avoids misunderstandings and sets out the expectations of the parents. Contracts will differ according to the individual requirements of parents and the type of nanny they employ. A resident nanny contract will require more detail than a daily nanny contract.

MAKE SURE THE CONTRACT INCLUDES

- Name and address of employer
- Name of employee and job title
- Date for the start of employment
- Nanny duties
- Salary expressed as a weekly, monthly or annual amount; state if this is a net or gross amount
- Normal hours of work
- Payment of expenses incurred while carrying out nanny duties
- Use of any car with regard to carrying out nanny duties
- A statement setting out employer house rules
- Confidentiality agreement
- Arrangements for sick pay
- Holiday entitlement
- Pension scheme (if any)
- Dismissal and disciplinary procedures, including a grievance procedure
- Termination and notice periods and any probationary period of employment

SALARY

Parents who wish to know what the 'going rate' is for a nanny's salary are advised to look in a professional magazine, such as *Nursery World*, or to phone a local nanny agency.

EXPENSES

Expenses payable to a nanny are those incurred in the course of childcare duties and that have been previously approved by the employer. It is wise for parents to explain what they regard as everyday expenses and for which they only require a receipt, such as supermarket bills for the children's meals, as opposed to expenses that need prior approval, such as buying the children's clothes. In this way, parents will have some input on the important purchases made on their behalf. A daily recording of all expenses needs to be made in a family diary (*see page 87 for more information on the family diary*) together with the relevant receipts.

NB: *All of the above information is a guide – it is very important for employers to check the information for themselves and to make best use of reputable organisations for specialist advice to be certain that they comply with current legislation.*

CHAPTER 5

NANNY MANAGEMENT

*It is very understandable if parents feel that once they
have successfully recruited their nanny most of their work
is done. However, this is not so! The energy and hard work
put in by parents at this point will hopefully be rewarded
by a professional, successful, trusting and long-lived
nanny/employer relationship. During the period between
the appointment and the actual start of the job there may
be many adjustments to be made by parents, children
and, if relevant, their existing nanny.*

*The relationship between a nanny and employer is a
unique one as it is both professional and personal.
The employer has to work out what the details of the
working relationship will be and managing the
relationship is crucial – letting things drift and avoiding
tackling any tricky issues will only lead to difficulties,
perhaps ending the relationship prematurely.*

72

*This chapter will consider some of the management
issues of which parents need to be aware:*

- *Preparing to welcome your nanny*
- *The first week of employment*
- *Managing a unique working relationship*
- *Guidelines for the future*

PREPARING TO WELCOME YOUR NANNY

The work that is put in during the preparatory period will be amply repaid when your nanny begins work. You are likely to have a month to prepare as this is approximately the time that a nanny would have to give notice in a previous post or the time that might be left for a training course to be completed.

One of the most important things to do is to recognise that your family life and perhaps your personal life will change with the arrival of your nanny. This is particularly the case when a family employs a nanny for the first time and it is a resident position. However, change will also be apparent when any new nanny arrives, as a new personality with personal opinions and characteristics will inevitably have an impact on family life – hopefully for the better. At the beginning of the employment it may seem as though you are living with a stranger in your home and both parents and nanny will be a little anxious, wanting to make good first impressions.

AGENCY MATTERS

Be certain that the agency has carried out all the necessary checks, such as the CRB check and the qualification check, and that you have paid the agency fee. It is also a good idea to give agency staff some feedback on the way that they have supported you in the search for your nanny. Remember to confirm the salary and the contents of the contract. Read the job description again and make certain that nothing important has been omitted. Confirm the start date and be clear if, for a resident post, you wish your nanny to turn up a day early, ready to start work the day after. If you have already discussed holiday dates or business travel confirm that these have been understood. You may have told your nanny that a valid passport and certain vaccinations are required as there is travel shortly after the post begins; if this is the case, now is the time to check that this is being carried out. Do not leave it until the nanny arrives on your doorstep.

NANNY ACCOMMODATION

'Spring clean' the accommodation before the arrival of your nanny. For a resident nanny, his or her accommodation is very important as a bolt-hole in his or her off-duty hours. Ensure that the accommodation is as comfortable and homely as is possible.

A nanny will either need a bathroom of his or her own or one shared with the children. Most nannies would prefer not to share a bathroom with their employers. Parents need to respect the nanny's privacy and not expect to be able to go into the room at any time. The children should also be taught to respect the privacy of the nanny. Your nanny will want to watch television, listen to music, relax, have friends around (with the family's permission), all without disturbing the rest of the family.

Self-contained accommodation can be very attractive to a nanny but this is not always possible. Where it is, it does give the nanny more of a sense of being 'off duty' and employers will have greater privacy and can reasonably expect their nanny to use the accommodation each evening and at weekends, which is of benefit to everyone.

A resident nanny will probably arrive with a lot of luggage, including a large amount of equipment ready for the children's creative activities. Make sure there is plenty of storage, as living among clutter is not conducive to a well-planned and organised day. It is entirely reasonable to expect your nanny to keep the room clean and tidy. It is still part of your home, and the nanny's attitude towards it is a reflection of the way he or she works. A non-resident nanny would also appreciate a place to put her personal belongings while 'on duty'.

FAMILY LIFESTYLE

Getting to know the children will be a high priority for the nanny, but getting to know the way the family functions is also an important part of settling in. If you have requirements relating to lifestyle, culture or religion these should have been discussed at interview. Now is the time to think about these requirements from a practical viewpoint. An example of this might be the way in which the food is prepared and cooked: your new nanny might be a vegetarian but your family possibly is not and you may expect meals to be prepared using meat and meat products; or a family might follow a vegan diet and your new nanny might need some practical help preparing meals and using vegan ingredients such as tofu; or family members may follow a particular religion, e.g. Islam, and therefore do not eat pork and pork products. Be clear as to your requirements about what you wish your children to eat and be prepared to guide your nanny through these requirements in the early stages of the job. It is essential to remember to tell your nanny about any foods to which the children are allergic; have this written down as it is very important information.

If a parent is going to be working from home, lay down some rules. Do you wish to remain undisturbed during working hours or are you happy to be involved with the children at mealtimes?

Are you happy for nanny friends and their charges to be invited to your home or do you wish to restrict the numbers and the frequency of days? Decide beforehand how you want your children's days to be organised and then you will be ready to explain to your nanny the preferred way of working.

THE NANNY CAR

If you are providing your nanny with a car for nanny duties, make sure that it is taxed and appropriately insured, fully serviced and has properly fitted child car seats; you should be prepared to show your nanny how the car seats are properly used. The car should be sparkling clean and tell your nanny that this is the way that you wish it to remain. Note any scratches or dents and tell your nanny that you are aware of these and that you expect to be kept informed of any similar mishaps and, obviously, any accidents. Tell your nanny that you do not wish other people's children to be driven in your car unless their parents have contacted you to give their permission. All children will need to use the appropriate car seat or seat belt on every single journey. (*See also page 81.*)

PREPARING YOUR CHILDREN

The children may make their feelings about their new nanny very clear. If they miss their previous nanny very much and feel very vulnerable and puzzled, their behaviour can appear to be anything but welcoming. A qualified nanny will understand the reasons for their behaviour and should be able to manage the situation effectively. The parents' role in this situation is to give support to the nanny, to understand the children's reactions and to arrange some of their favourite activities that they can undertake with the nanny. If there are any changes to be made from the way the previous nanny worked explain these to the children and take responsibility for these new changes and start them as soon as possible so that the children become used to them. If it is the first time that your children have been looked after by a nanny be sure to emphasise the fun they will have, the activities they can enjoy and reassure them that you will still be around and look forward to hearing about their adventures!

True life stories: A warm welcome

Three-year-old twins Charlotte and Emily were really looking forward to seeing Tilly. Their mother, Helen, had told them that Tilly was to be their nanny and would arrive on Monday morning, which was the start of their half-term holiday. Helen had arranged to take four days' leave from work to help Tilly settle in and to help the twins make the gradual transition from having a parent around the home all day to sharing their care with their mother and their nanny. Helen also wanted to make sure that Tilly met the twins' friends and the nursery-school staff as Tilly would be responsible for taking them and collecting them from nursery school. Helen had also told them that Tilly would take them swimming, to ballet and to the other places that they liked to go. Charlotte and Emily thought that Tilly would be fun and they had collected some flowers from the garden to put in her bedroom. They had also made a 'welcome card' and some gingerbread biscuits.
Helen had prepared them well and was hopeful that everyone would enjoy the new experience.

- Have banking arrangements been set up to pay the nanny salary?
- Does the nanny accommodation look homely and welcoming?

- Is the nanny car 'ready to go'?
- Have nursery staff and other relevant people been informed of the nanny's arrival?

THE FIRST WEEK OF EMPLOYMENT

It is during this first week of the nanny's employment that standards are set and boundaries established. If at all possible, try to take some leave so that the new nanny works alongside you for a week or at least for a few days. This is a valuable time to get to know your nanny and to observe the interaction between nanny and children. Parents could delegate this important handover to the previous nanny but on some occasions this will result in bad habits being passed from one nanny to another. When Emily Ward founded the Norland College in 1892, one of her reasons for doing so was her belief that the training of a nanny should not lie in the hands of a more senior nanny working in the household as both good and bad traits in the skills, knowledge and attitudes of one nanny could be passed onto her more junior counterpart. Ward believed that the care and education of young children was too important to be tackled in this haphazard way, hence the foundation of a formal training college.

An efficient and experienced nanny will gain information from shadowing the parent so, whenever possible, try to ensure that parent and nanny work alongside each other in the first few days of the settling-in process. In this situation the nanny will gain far more than factual information. It is possible to absorb the approach taken by the parents, to find out what is really important and which things are less so. The children can see both nanny and parents happily working together and hopefully adopting similar attitudes to the positive management of the children's behaviour. Children may also have the opportunity to notice that both nanny and parent have the same answer to the classic 'wanting the chocolate biscuit' situation! Agreeing policies in advance for these situations is extremely useful.

The first week can be a tricky time for everyone and some safe topics of conversation can include your children, members of your family, such as grandparents, and the various activities that your children enjoy. You will have to gauge how forthcoming your nanny is about his or her family and his or her previous nanny experiences and be guided by this as to the direction of conversation. However, if you have confidentiality high on your agenda for a 'perfect nanny' be discreet in your conversations.

You are establishing your relationship at this time and direction needs to be given as to how you want your nanny to refer to you. In most informal posts employers are now happy to be referred to by their first name but in other situations parents do not feel that this is appropriate. Parents have to work out if they are happy for the working relationship to be both professional and friendly, perhaps working as colleagues in a small 'team' environment. Just tell your nanny what you want.

If you employ other staff in your home, explain to your nanny the role of each member of staff and where the nanny's role dovetails into the family organisation. As mentioned on page 27 in Chapter 3, a list of 'Who does what and when' is a good guideline. Some tips to the nanny as to how to cope with any 'unusual' characters would also be particularly helpful and may save some household unrest!

THE WEEKLY ROUTINE

In the first week, it is very helpful to make clear who is 'in charge' for the week. Is it the parent or the nanny? Is it the previous nanny or the new nanny? This is necessary so that the children are clear as to who is making the decisions and who is in a supporting role. A united front is essential regardless of who is in charge.

Writing out the main points of the weekly routine can be helpful. You will already have discussed the daily routine and should also expect your nanny to want to make some minor changes with your agreement.

THE WEEKLY ROUTINE

Monday morning
Mrs Jones arrives at 9am to clean the bedrooms and the bathrooms; leaves at midday. You are responsible for James's bedroom and bathroom as well as your own.
Afternoon
James swims; he needs armbands. Your membership has been arranged.

Tuesday morning
James to pre-school for 9.15am; remember his book bag. This is a good time to clean and tidy the playroom and sort out the toys and books. Collect James at 12.30pm.

Wednesday morning
This is a good time to do some cooking, messy play or creative play activities with James as Mrs Jones is not in and you can use the kitchen.

Wednesday afternoon
James loves story time at the library; it starts at 2pm. Library tickets are in the kitchen drawer.

Thursday morning
James to pre-school for 9.15am; collect James at 12.30pm. You could cook some meals for James that could be put in the freezer – organic ingredients only please!

Friday morning
Mrs Jones arrives at 9am; she leaves at midday. Please can you make sure that all of James's clothes are laundered and ironed and put away?
Afternoon
James likes to go to the park. He often meets Harry and Beth and they are fine to play together.

Try to make the first week as close as possible to what will be the normal weekly routine. If there are children to be collected from nursery school make this a joint effort as the nanny can then learn the route, meet the staff and perhaps some other parents and children with whom you might be friendly. On some occasions it will also be an opportunity for your nanny to meet other nannies and this might help to reduce the sense of isolation if your nanny is new to the area or if it is a first job.

If walking the dog is part of the contractual duties, ensure that this happens with you pointing out some good routes and demonstrating how you want your dog to be handled.

Start putting some entries into the family diary (*see page 87*) so that your nanny is encouraged to do the same.

MEALTIMES

Mealtimes are important occasions and it is in the first week that parents can provide firm guidance as to what they want their nanny to do. Providing a role model is important: if you wish your children to have home-cooked meals using all organic ingredients, it is not a good idea to buy in a bagful of frozen meals from the local supermarket saying, 'This is what we will do this week but next week all freshly cooked meals, please!' A nanny in this situation could feel some resentment that home-cooked, organic meals are only a high priority when the nanny is responsible! This is a not a good start nor a message of consistency.

A mealtime is also the occasion to set the standard for acceptable manners and politeness. The children may not feel particularly helpful at this point and may be thinking of ways of demonstrating how much they miss their previous nanny. Remain calm and firmly establish your usual boundaries, thus informing the nanny what you expect, even if on this occasion it appears anything but an enjoyable social mealtime. Establish what your attitudes are to eating habits and expect the nanny to follow.

USE OF THE CAR

In the handover period it is a good idea for the nanny to go on some solo journeys while you look after the children. Your nanny most probably has to get used to a different car and to driving in an unfamiliar area. Provide the nanny with some time to get used to the car and to do some practice runs to nursery and other places to which your children travel. It is better for your nanny to learn about the car and the locality without having your children in the car for the first few journeys. After a few days accompany the nanny on some routine journeys. Satisfy yourself that your nanny is a safe driver and is competent to take your children in the car.

PUNCTUALITY

You need to know that your nanny will collect the children promptly and that a daily nanny will turn up for work in plenty of time for you to leave for work. During the first week be alert for any signs of lateness and address it promptly, but be sympathetic to any genuine reason. Do not accept 'traffic' as a reason, as your nanny will have to realise that more time will have to be allowed for her daily journey to your house. This is an important aspect of the job to emphasise, as it could have a big impact on your own job. When there are the occasional times of late arrival or, in the case of sickness, non-appearance, make sure that your nanny knows you need as much notice as possible to make other arrangements, which is not always easy.

DRESS CODE

In the days when a nanny had a uniform the matter of what a nanny wore was less complicated. It revolved around keeping the uniform clean and pressed and worn smartly. Now it is less easy: as an employer, the parent needs to decide what is acceptable for the nanny to wear when 'on duty'. Some employers decide that jeans are not appropriate, while others find this acceptable. A dress code should have been discussed at interview, and during the first week a parent will be able to see the practical implementation of the given guidelines. If, as an employer, you feel uncomfortable about very skimpy tops or low-slung trousers now is the time to say so as there will be a tendency for the nanny to relax the dress code as the weeks go by. Your nanny should dress appropriately for a professional role and represent your family in any way that you find appropriate. Being clear about what you expect during this first week will make it easier for you to address tricky problems in the future! Remember, consistency and communication are the key.

HOUSEHOLD MATTERS

The 'leaving the house' routine is very often the basis of many parent/nanny conflicts. The parent is paranoid about locking all doors and windows and putting the burglar alarm on, but perhaps the nanny has not been used to this regime in either her own or her parents' home. Make sure to follow your own routine on every occasion that you leave the house with your nanny and the children. Explain the alarm system and the number code for any door lock. You may double-lock your door – if so, remind your nanny about the importance of doing this. If you want the door chain to be used make sure that you also use it. After the first day leave the nanny to do all the checks but give him or her plenty of

AND FINALLY

If you have agreed to pay your nanny on a weekly basis, make very certain that you do so at the end of the first week. You will have had to previously set up the banking arrangements together with those for tax and national insurance. Remember that your nanny must also have a payslip. It would be very demoralizing, regardless of the excuse, for all of your hard work in the first week to be ruined by the non-appearance of the weekly salary!

time and do not pressurize – it takes time to learn someone else's routines and it does not help to have someone standing over you.

During this first week try to use as many household appliances as possible. It is an opportunity for the nanny to work out how to use the machines with the parent being a helpful guide throughout.

MANAGING A UNIQUE WORKING RELATIONSHIP

Many people choose to employ a nanny because either one or both parents are working in professional environments, perhaps where they have significant responsibility both for employees and various projects. Their work often requires good time-management skills, delegation and effective communication. Similarly, these skills are needed when employing a nanny. As with many working relationships, it requires effort and energy by all parties to achieve a successful outcome. If working parents are to pursue their careers competently and professionally they need reliable childcare. For working parents, it can be said that behind every successful career there is a totally supportive and respected nanny!

Employers are very dependent on their nanny and it is this dependency that brings with it issues that may not be present in other working relationships. In other working environments the manager may have to discuss with the employee work that is of an unsatisfactory standard, then both parties go home and start again after the weekend break. For a resident nanny, this is not always possible. It must be remembered and respected that for the resident nanny, his or her place of work is not left at 5pm, the nanny simply goes 'off duty'. Remaining in the employer's home can often mean that the nanny cannot leave behind all the stresses and strains of the working day. Where there has been a serious lapse in standards and the nanny takes exception to the discussion and decides to resign immediately, the family are left in a crisis without any childcare. Although this does not happen often, when it does the parents are left with a dilemma. Should time be taken away from work to look after the children and find a replacement nanny? Or are there relatives close by who are able to help out on a temporary

83

basis? Neither solution is ideal, and so the unwelcome possibility of the nanny leaving can often inhibit communication and cause some unsatisfactory situations to remain unaddressed.

GIVING FEEDBACK

As with other employees, the nanny needs feedback on how he or she is performing the job. Initially, this should be on a weekly basis while everyone settles into the new situation. Later, this could become monthly, followed by a more formal six-monthly and then annual appraisals. At the start of their new post, most nannies will want to work in a way that meets parents' expectations and will need feedback to know the parents' wishes. Remember that feedback needs to include positive points as well as addressing areas that need to be developed and improved. Remember that nannies will consider themselves professional practitioners bringing knowledge and skills to their job, expertise which they would wish to be respected by their employers.

Where there are small points for improvement, this needs to be communicated promptly and calmly, conveying what needs to happen in the future and acknowledging the areas where the nanny has worked well. For more important points, time will have to be made for a fuller discussion when both the nanny and the employer can explore their different viewpoints to agree a way forward. On these occasions it is important to be able to concentrate on the matters to be discussed, therefore the conversation needs to be held when the children are in bed or being looked after by someone other then the nanny. Rather than gathering issues for discussion, which can lead to them becoming out of proportion and causing great anxiety, it is far better to have a regular meeting time perhaps once every fortnight when both good and not-so-good points can be raised by both nanny and employer. Where there is honest and constructive discussion, the relationship becomes stronger, mutual respect develops and trust grows. And it is this type of relationship that truly benefits the children.

When you have scheduled a more formal appraisal of your nanny's work, make certain that you have given advance notification and that the time is convenient for everyone.

SOME POINTS TO THINK ABOUT FOR AN APPRAISAL

- The job description provides the basis for employer expectations and standards of work
- Make sure there are no distractions when carrying out an appraisal
- Appraisals enable good work to be acknowledged as well as areas for development identified
- Listening is an important part of the appraisal process
- Appraisal is a two-way process, with the views of all parties considered
- Appraisal is an opportunity for difficulties to be raised in a supportive environment
- Give the nanny the opportunity to self-assess his or her work
- Parents needs to be clear about any improvements needed and the ways in which they will support their nanny to achieve these
- Agree the date for any desired improvement to be reviewed
- End the appraisal discussion on a positive note

COMMUNICATION

If asked to identify the key ingredient of a successful and long-lasting nanny/parent relationship, the answer would have to be effective communication. This will not come as a surprise to many parents but the question remains as to how this is to be achieved – there are so many things that need to be communicated to the new nanny! Organisation is the key.

Some factual aspects of the job can be written down prior to the nanny's arrival. Others need communicating with more detail and are best done verbally, giving the nanny the chance to clarify and the parent to add explanation, and to convey that these things are really very important and the reasons why. However, it is important to remember at the start of any new job that only so much information can be taken in at any one time. Some points will need to be repeated over time and others added once the really important information has been absorbed. Parents need to be approachable so that if the nanny does not understand anything, it is perfectly acceptable to ask questions once and even twice!

If you make clear what the boundaries and non-negotiable matters are, everybody is certain and there are no embarrassing situations. For example, if there are parts of the house that are out of bounds be very clear, or if you have precious ornaments point these out.

If at any time you sense a slightly hostile atmosphere, think carefully why this might be and discuss it as soon as possible so there are no frosty times. This is another reason why the fortnightly or, preferably, weekly meeting is a good idea. A regular forum avoids problem situations dragging on. Keep to the arranged meeting even if sometimes both parties say they have nothing to discuss. These meetings can focus on what is going well and do not always have to be held to discuss problems.

IMPORTANT INFORMATION TO WRITE DOWN

- Parent contact numbers – work and mobile
- Emergency arrangements: doctor and hospital phone numbers and travel directions
- Written permission for your nanny to give your children particular types of medicine and where you wish this to be recorded

- Arrangements for locking the house and to set the burglar alarm
- Where spare sets of keys are held
- Car breakdown and insurance information
- Instructions for using all domestic and household appliances

THE FAMILY DIARY

Keeping a written family diary is another useful communication tool, especially for the resident nanny. The diary can do far more than merely record events on certain dates. Parents can write in appointments for the children that the nanny needs to keep, such as check-ups at the dentist, as well as their own important business commitments and when they will be late back from work. The nanny can put in nursery/parent open evenings and her own important social events or any special requests for family events.

The diary gives everybody the opportunity to communicate well in advance for planned events and minimises those times when there is a conflict of interest. The diary only works well when the parents and nanny contribute and give full information.

If the children are visiting their friends to play, the nanny should, on the first occasion, write down the address and contact details, including those of the friends' parents, so that both sets of parents can communicate if they wish to. The diary is also a means of the parent monitoring if the children are doing too much socialising or not enough. Be clear about the amount of socialising you want for your children, as well as with whom you want your children to socialise. It is the responsibility of the nanny to fit in with what the parent wishes.

Ask your nanny to also make brief notes about what the children have done during the day and what activities or outings they might have particularly enjoyed. This will enable parents to feel in touch with their children and to carry on some relevant conversation on their return from work. At the weekend, you may wish to extend some of the activities, perhaps going with the children to the library or the bookshop to choose some relevant books. Child development observation notes can also be written in the diary. A qualified nanny will have spent much of his or her training course carrying out child development observations and may enjoy sharing his or her knowledge of children's development with parents.

True life stories: A working diary

When Peter began his job working as a resident nanny in Newcastle, he suggested to his employer that they both contribute to a 'working diary', as this had proved very useful in his previous employment. Jo, his employer, thought this could be a good idea and said that she would be happy to try it out. Peter asked her to put in the days she would be working away from the office and possibly late home. He particularly wanted to know when she would have to stay away from home overnight. This was important information for him as on these occasions he would not be able to make his own social arrangements. He also wanted to let Jo know in advance when he needed to keep some evenings free to attend some basketball matches and to celebrate his birthday. Peter also wrote information in the diary about the children's activities and Jo put in reminders about dental visits and hairdressing appointments. The system worked very well and both Jo and Peter decided to continue with it. Both Jo and Peter thought that when they regularly completed the diary it helped both of them to work more efficiently.

MAINTAINING A PROFESSIONAL RELATIONSHIP

Strangely, as all parties settle in to having the new nanny and communication is effective, it can bring about situations where, as the working relationship becomes closer and a friendship develops, it inhibits the role of the employer. When praise is given there is no problem, but when the employer feels that there are matters of unsatisfactory standards of work to be discussed, there is a reluctance to do this as it is felt that the good working relationship could be upset and the nanny could feel offended.

The crucial thing to remember is that this relationship is a professional one with the employee needing to carry out the nanny role to certain standards, which should never be allowed to slip in terms of the children's safety and well-being. Always keep your children's interests in mind and this thought will support you if needing to make clear your views on an unacceptable standard of work. However, always give support, and when standards improve make sure that you tell your nanny that you have noticed the improvement. It is also true to say that in a long-term successful employment, the nanny, too, can find it difficult to raise certain issues, such as pay.

LISTEN TO YOUR CHILDREN

It is absolutely essential to listen to your children. Children who are being looked after by a nanny for the first time may naturally feel upset with this change. Perhaps they have been cared for by one of their parents for a long time and miss this contact. Parents who have been in this situation may also miss their children and experience feelings of guilt at returning to work. All of these feelings are very understandable and an experienced nanny will have come across these situations quite frequently. If you are a new nanny employer, give yourself time to adjust to the new situation and if you discuss it with friends in similar circumstances you will find that you are not alone in feeling the way you do!

For children old enough to understand, tell them about their change of carer and the reasons for it. Explain why people change jobs perhaps, if relevant, using yourself as an example. Children worry that the reason that the carer is leaving is due to something they have or have not done. Reassure the children that there are no further changes on the horizon and remind them of the very pleasant nanny who is to look after them and who, hopefully, they have met. If applicable, and possible, tell the children that the 'old' nanny will come to their birthday parties or visit before Christmas, but do not promise anything that you do not want or that is not feasible for either the family or the nanny.

Listen to what your children are telling you about the new nanny and about the things they do together. If your children are not forthcoming do not be anxious too soon as it does take some children a long time to be able to let go of their old carer and welcome their new one. If, however, your children remain uncommunicative, think why this might be so and ask other parents, friends and adults who frequent places that the children visit how they seem when with their new nanny.

With babies and very young children who find it difficult to understand the changes, it is important to understand the reasons for their puzzlement and confusion. Try to be reassuring with plenty of hugs, cuddles and stories. Keep consistently to the daily routine and make every effort to be home for bedtime and not to work overnight away from home. All children thrive in a loving environment and need security. A change of carer can be a difficult time for all concerned, but when everybody works hard and communicates well the possible turmoil for children is reduced.

EFFECTIVE COMMUNICATION WITH YOUR NANNY

- Concentrate on what is being communicated and remove interruptions
- Be clear about what you want to say and listen actively
- Observe body language: is the non-verbal communication in tune with what is being said? If not, think why
- If non-negotiable boundaries are being pressured, say 'No' and establish the boundaries again
- Remember the power of justified praise – if your nanny is doing a good job, say so!
- Avoid interrupting your nanny, listen and be patient
- Problems raised by your nanny do not necessarily mean parents are being personally criticised
- Be prepared to negotiate and to change your views – remember, your nanny is also a professional
- Try to understand the reasons for what is being said
- Disagree, if necessary, but always calmly and politely, never rudely or aggressively
- Summarise what your views are and also the opinion of your nanny
- Decide on a way forward; if necessary, arrange another meeting
- Try to end on a positive note

GUIDELINES FOR THE FUTURE

Building trust and a professional relationship begins at the start of employment and continues from there. The use of a 'nanny cam' to record the behaviour of a nanny has some supporters but it is reasonable to ask that if an employer feels it necessary to install a camera, can the relationship be one of trust and openness? A nanny has to manage many difficult situations and the parent has to have trust that these situations will be dealt with appropriately – that is, after all, why you have employed a professional nanny. Trust has to be earned and given and worked at by all parties.

MANAGING CHILDREN'S BEHAVIOUR

You will have told your nanny at the interview stage that on no occasion will there ever be a reason for your child to be smacked, but now is the time for you as the parent to be clear about what sanctions connected with unwanted behaviour there are for your nanny to use, hopefully, on just a few occasions. You will need to explain what boundaries are set for your children. Of course, whatever approach you describe should be the same one that you use with your child when necessary. For any approach to be successful and understood by the child it has to have total consistency and be appropriate to the child's age and stage of development.

Knowledge of child development

An important aspect of any qualified childcare practitioner's training course will be the focus on child development. Any approach to managing a child's behaviour should be grounded in an understanding of child development. How a child's behaviour is managed is affected by what a child can understand and actually do. For example, some children aged about two years may have tantrums and a range of behaviours that are very frustrating to the adult caring for them. The reason why children in that age group often throw tantrums is that their language ability is not always sufficiently developed to be able to express clearly to the adult what they may or may not want to do. Their feelings are very strong at this age and can quickly overwhelm them and everybody in the vicinity! Children can find it intensely frustrating that the adult cannot understand their needs. As the child's language ability progresses, the frustration and the accompanying tantrums decrease. When a nanny or parent understands this aspect of development the behaviour is also more understandable and more effort can be made to prevent an outburst together with trying to understand what the child is communicating.

How your nanny can manage children's behaviour

For a two-year-old, it is better to try to use distraction or an alternative activity rather than confrontation. For older children, the best approach is to keep the child busy with interesting and appropriate activities, and when unwanted behaviour has to be managed, explain carefully why this behaviour is unacceptable together with a simple statement as to what should have happened.

As a parent you need to be a role model for the nanny as well as the child. If shouting is used as one means of managing unwanted behaviour it should come as no surprise if you observe both the nanny and the child shouting at each other. It is an important part of any approach for the parent and the nanny to make the child aware that it is the behaviour that is unwanted and never the child. Children need to know that they will always be loved no matter what happens and very often a particularly difficult time of tantrums and frustration will be ended with a cuddle and a hug and lots of reassuring words.

As children become older, the explanation of why some behaviour is unacceptable gains in importance. If a child is aggressive, he or she can be helped to understand why the behaviour is hurtful and upsetting to the other child and to think what it would be like to be on the receiving end. Sometimes aggression occurs because the concept of sharing is not understood or because boredom has set in or the child feels confined. Depending on the reason for the aggression, the child could be offered the opportunity to go outside and take part in a more physical game, making sure that there is lots of equipment for everyone.

A caring and competent nanny should be able to handle all these situations skilfully and calmly. If you are observing the nanny dealing with one of these situations you should be able to watch while a quiet explanation takes place at the child's level with eye contact maintained and positive body language and gestures. With this positive, consistent approach there should also be a commitment to praising good behaviour. On some occasions it can be better to ignore the unwanted behaviour and to find something that can be justifiably praised. If a child learns that the only way to gain adult attention is to hit or swear or bite then in the child's eyes these behaviours gain in importance. What we want to achieve is for the child to gain social skills and behaviours that enable them to cooperate with friends and to be happy and contented people.

You should make sure that your nanny knows that you want to be kept informed about any significant bouts of difficult behaviour together with the reasons for it and the way it was handled. A short note in the family diary will be sufficient and gives the parent the chance to see any particular patterns building and to consider whether it is something that needs to be addressed further.

CHAPTER 6

THE NANNY'S PERSPECTIVE

Parents may wonder why, in a book to help them find the perfect nanny, there is a chapter that looks at employment from the perspective of a nanny. Well, the ability to understand the nanny's perspective helps the parent and the nanny to work towards a long and successful partnership. If a parent can understand what is important to a nanny and why, it will help the nanny to settle into the job and also help the employer avoid inadvertently acting in a negative way that results in the nanny's resignation.

The importance of valuing the knowledge and expertise of the qualified practitioner cannot be overemphasised. As a parent and employer, you have made the choice about who you will trust to work with you to care and educate your young children, so it is important to demonstrate the value you place in your nanny's professional expertise.

This chapter will enable parents to understand more about their nanny's expectations and in so doing to work towards success.

- *What are the expectations of a nanny?*
- *How to build a long-lasting relationship*
- *Developing the nanny's role*

WHAT ARE THE EXPECTATIONS OF A NANNY?

Very simply, the expectations of a nanny can be summed up by the thought: 'Is the job as it was described at the interview and in the job description?'. Before taking up the position the nanny will have drawn up a picture of what he or she thinks the job will entail, how he or she will be treated and how the employer–employee relationship is likely to develop. It is helpful for an employer to have an insight as to why a particular job may appeal.

True life stories: Choosing a family

Louisa recalls why she chose her job:

'I took the view that the process was as much about me choosing the employer as them selecting me. I took everything into account – for example their attitude to discipline, the quality of the accommodation, and their relationship with each other as parents. I knew I wanted to work for this family almost immediately, but the decision was made much easier for me when I had my stay-over visit. After dinner, Janine told her husband that he would be doing the washing up and babysitting, so that she could take me out to show me the area. It was a warm June evening and she put the roof of her car down and drove me around all the sights of London – "There's St Paul's Cathedral … There's Big Ben" – it was absolutely brilliant.'

The choice of job will not only be made on first impressions but also based on a combination of previous childcare and nanny experience, the interview experiences and the conversations about the job that have previously taken place. The nanny will create an idea of the job in her head. Sometimes the expectations of both the nanny and the parent are not explicitly expressed and are unspoken but assumed. This type of unspoken agreement can be described as a 'psychological' contract.

THE PSYCHOLOGICAL CONTRACT

This type of 'contract' is a subjective, unwritten agreement, which can influence an employee's beliefs about how the employment should be conducted and consequently influence the employee's behaviour. Where all is well in the job and the nanny is satisfied that all 'terms and conditions' are being met there are few, if any, difficulties. Where there is a perception on the part of the nanny that much of the content of the contract remains unmet, there is often a change in the nanny's standard of work as well as in attitude and well-being. However, as the issues remain unspoken, the employer can find it difficult to ascertain the reasons for these changes in the nanny. In a young and perhaps inexperienced nanny, expectations may be based on an 'ideal world' scenario rather than on reality; the nanny may expect a great deal from the employer and be dissatisfied when the employer is not faultless.

A frequent example of this is when the nanny feels that regular praise and recognition should be a normal, almost daily, event. The employer, often a very busy person with a whole range of business responsibilities, regards the standard of the nanny's work being just as it should be and not one requiring daily acknowledgement or praise. Over time, the nanny feels that the work is not valued and the picture built up about this 'ideal employer' is somewhat dented. Essential parts of the psychological contract involve trust and loyalty and this contract is thought to be 'broken' when trust and loyalty are diminished. Very often the breaking of the psychological contract is due to poor communication and a lack of empathy by both parties.

BREAKING THE PSYCHOLOGICAL CONTRACT CAN RESULT IN:

- The sudden departure of the nanny who feels disillusioned and unable to voice concerns
- A period of silence on the part of the nanny, who hopes that things will improve without any action being taken
- A withdrawal of goodwill by the nanny who feels, rightly or wrongly, a sense of injustice
- A feeling of being undervalued resulting in a demoralised nanny

In all of the above situations, the employer must listen and discuss with the nanny the reasons for dissatisfaction and where appropriate change things to more closely match the nanny's expectations. Gently inquire about what the expectations were and why this is the case. Where change is not possible, it is very important to explain why this is so, listen again to the nanny's expectations and to agree another time to discuss matters, hopefully to see some improvement. Try not to back the nanny into a corner and leave no room for manoeuvre or negotiation. If small changes can be made this is very often sufficient to regain the status quo and for normal relationships and goodwill to be restored.

A more easily understood contract is the one that is drawn up and signed by both parties at the beginning of the employment. This contract sets out clearly what is expected from the employer in terms of the nanny's 'big four'.

THE BIG FOUR – PAY, PERKS, WORKING HOURS AND HOLIDAY

Any discussion among nannies regarding why they chose their position will eventually centre on one or all of the 'big four'. Salary, the perks of the post, the hours of work and holiday arrangements will be top of the agenda. The discussion may also revolve round other reasons, such as thinking there will be a good relationship based on mutual respect with the parents, but the 'big four' will always be compared and commented on. If parents understand the importance of these criteria to their nanny they will know that, whenever possible, these should be as attractive as possible within the boundary of what is affordable and sustainable.

Pay

When it comes to the nanny's pay, issues of sustainability are important as the nanny will, reasonably, expect regular salary increases. If the family finances cannot comfortably afford the nanny's salary it is quite possible that resentment will set in. Parents may ask themselves why they are working so hard to pay the salary when there is very little money left over, after all other financial commitments are met. It is important to remember that with a resident nanny, the employer will incur additional costs, such as those for food, travel and phone.

True life stories: Worth the wait

Gilly was very experienced, having worked as a nanny for eight years for two different families. She decided that she wished to gain some additional experience and wanted to work for a family where there would be a newborn baby.

Gilly contacted an agency and discussed her requirements. The agency sent her several job descriptions, as they were keen to place her. Gilly had decided that she would not be pressurised and read each job description carefully, making some notes using the headings: pay, perks, working hours and holidays. These helped her to be clear about what she was looking for. After nine weeks, she was sent a job with a newborn baby where the employers were prepared to recognise the long working hours through a very good salary. There were no real 'perks' attached to the job but Gilly thought that with a good salary she could pay for a gym membership and a decent car if she wanted to! She applied for the job and was successful. She was very happy with her salary and with the family for whom she had chosen to work.

THE NANNY PERSPECTIVE – SALARY

- The nanny expects the salary to be at least the 'going rate' for the area
- The salary should be weighted according to experience, qualifications and local demand
- Paying a proper salary will be rewarded by loyalty and commitment
- The salary should be increased if there are extra demands, such as looking after a young baby
- An improvement in salary should be seen if longer hours are worked than originally agreed
- Paying a low salary is very short-sighted

Perks

The starting point for the nanny as regards the perks of the job will be what the employer has written in the job description or contract or described at the interview. Training-college staff, careers advisers and agency staff will tell a nanny many times not to accept any job based on the perks. However, parents are sometimes tempted to emphasise these perks in order to glamorise the job to find their perfect nanny, and many inexperienced or newly qualified nannies will be tempted by these perks (even though they will frequently say that this was not the case).

THE NANNY PERSPECTIVE – PERKS

- A nanny expects the perks of the job to be 'as described'
- A nanny views perks as an important part of the job-choice criteria
- When perks are promised in 'lieu of pay' an experienced nanny will be very wary
- An 'all paid for' attractive car for the exclusive use of the nanny, both on and off duty, is viewed as a worthwhile perk
- Membership of well-appointed health spas and tickets to exclusive events are also valued by a nanny

Working hours

The contract should state clearly what the agreed working hours should be but, as in many professional jobs, there is a degree of flexibility expected. Generally speaking, most nannies know this and are not unduly concerned about being flexible and working occasionally for a short time outside of their normal working hours. This is the case for both resident and daily nannies. However, nannies like as much notice as possible of any change in arrangements and expect not to be taken for granted. They also expect any previous arrangements honoured, especially those that have been noted in the family diary.

Nannies value their time away from the job and if 'off duty' do not wish to be phoned about insignificant matters, such as the location of an item of clothing. It is important for employers to respect this 'off-duty' time, especially for resident nannies when it can be too easy to ask a quick question that could wait until Monday morning. Non-resident nannies agree that they would rather come in a little earlier on a Monday than pop into their place of work at the weekend.

Holidays

Holidays are as important to nannies as to any other group of people and it is important that they do take all of their holiday allowance so that they can fully recharge their batteries. It is usual for the nanny to choose some weeks to take leave and for the employer to nominate other weeks.

One area that can cause particular dissatisfaction for nannies is when they are told that they will not be needed to work while their employer is on holiday or away for a few days and, therefore, will not be paid. Employers who take this action are not looking at the long-term view: the wish to retain their nanny. The view of most nannies is that they are available to work and should be paid.

Family holidays that involve taking a nanny to an exotic location can be an initial attraction to a job, particularly for inexperienced nannies. Employers need to remind the nanny that frequent overseas travel can be hard work and exhausting. Taking the nanny on the family holiday is a situation that needs to be handled sensitively by employers who should appreciate that childcare in unfamiliar surroundings can be very demanding and more exhausting than usual. Also, the nanny is working while others are relaxing and enjoying themselves. The nanny will, in turn, expect these difficult circumstances and the resulting hard work to be valued and recognised. It is a good idea for the employer to offer some extra time 'off duty', especially if there are social or sporting activities in which the nanny would like to participate. Experienced nannies tend to be fully aware of the demands of overseas childcare and may ask for accommodation separate from their charges.

HOW TO BUILD A LONG-LASTING RELATIONSHIP
RESPECT

This is the aspect most frequently mentioned by nannies when discussing what attracts them to staying with a particular employer. Being respected by an employer is also linked to knowing that an employer trusts a nanny and values his or her professional skills and expertise. This trust is usually gained over a period of time and a trained nanny will appreciate that trust has to be worked at while settling into each post.

When changes occur in the family, a nanny will want these to be fully discussed. Changes, such as a house move, a new baby or a divorce, have a significant effect on the role of the nanny and may require a new job description. It is part of respecting your nanny and trusting that, where necessary, confidentiality can be maintained, to ensure that any significant changes in the nanny role are discussed.

If anything has gone wrong at the employer's workplace, an employer should try to remember that it is not the fault of the nanny; while it is often helpful to chat through the day's events, it is not conducive to the parent–nanny relationship for the employer to re-run the day and its difficulties in a self-indulgent manner. Most nannies will want to appear sympathetic the first few times but will quickly tire of this.

As an employer it can often be helpful to think of what you pay your nanny as an investment in your family life. Paying a good salary that you can afford, together with looking after your nanny with regard to holidays and the working environment, means that you are showing that you value your nanny and appreciate how family life runs smoothly in part due to the way in which your children are cared for and are happy and contented. Your nanny will also feel more valued and is less likely to start looking for another job. Good, efficient, kind and capable nannies are very much sought after and will often receive tentative enquiries or a direct approach about whether or not they are looking for another job. Quite rightly, employers can expect loyalty and commitment but they also need to be aware that they must work hard at keeping their 'perfect nanny'.

HONESTY

Building a long-lasting relationship requires honesty in the relationship, but employers need to remember that when things go wrong it is how you handle them that affects your nanny. If your nanny has not acted as you would wish, politely explain what was wrong and how you want them to act in the future.

DEVELOPING THE NANNY'S ROLE

The way in which nannies can develop their role, with the support of their employer, can often play a part in their decision as to how long they wish to remain in a particular post. When a nanny has just qualified, he or she is reasonably happy to settle into the role, work hard, enjoy the company of the children and the parents in the knowledge that he or she is doing a good job and hope to get a good first reference. At some point in a nanny's career, he or she will wish to gain different experiences and, sometimes, to update his or her knowledge and gain more qualifications.

It is not always possible for an existing employer to meet requests for gaining new experience so a nanny has no alternative but to move on. There are, however, often some possibilities: as an employer it is always worth listening to the ideas of your nanny on this subject and then thinking about what you can do. Very often, if the children are attending pre-school for a couple of mornings each week, there is the possibility for a nanny to pursue a work-related interest during this time. Gaining different experiences is often the prelude to becoming even more employable, but usually if an employer can support his or her nanny in this way there is a definite increase in goodwill and motivation to stay. Any new experience will have to fit in with the nanny's existing responsibilities, but new experiences outside of the home may help to reduce any sense of isolation.

FURTHER EDUCATION

Some childcarers may want to gain additional qualifications for their own professional development. This can be quite demanding while working full time, but with the increase in distance learning

WAYS IN WHICH A NANNY CAN EXTEND HER EXPERIENCE

- Work for a family with children of different ages
- Gain experience looking after a newborn baby and mother
- Look after a child with special needs
- Care for twins, triplets or quads
- Work in a voluntary capacity in a pre-school or reception class
- Learn a language

courses it is a definite possibility. The Open University has an extensive range of childcare courses leading to many different levels of qualifications.

Employer support for the improvement of a nanny's education is a definite help. If the nanny is studying for a childcare-related qualification there may be a course requirement to carry out particular activities with children as well as the need to set aside several hours a week for study. On some occasions there may be the possibility for the nanny to attend a short course at the local children's centre to update a qualification such as first-aid. Short courses may also be offered in relation to the early years curriculum or to starting school; these types of courses will help any school-age children to make a smooth transition into formal education and settle happily into their new surroundings. By supporting and encouraging your nanny in the pursuit of knowledge both your children and the nanny will benefit.

CHAPTER 7

EARLY YEARS EDUCATION IN THE HOME

When parents and nanny are fully involved with a child's education, it provides an excellent introduction to learning. Nannies who are qualified practitioners know that they have a role to play by supporting children in their early learning experiences and closely involving parents by sharing their children's experiences with them.

A research project entitled Effective Provision of Pre-School Education (EPPE) carried out in 2004 showed that the quality of the home-learning environment had a far greater effect on children's learning and development than a parent's occupation, income or level of education. For busy parents, knowing that a nanny is providing appropriate learning opportunities and has the skills to promote the all-round development of their child can be a weight off their minds.

This chapter looks at the way in which a nanny can influence important aspects of children's early years education.

- *How a nanny can help children to learn*
- *Home-learning and your nanny*
- *Preparing children for school*
- *Encouraging play and learning*

HOW A NANNY CAN HELP CHILDREN TO LEARN

Nannies play a vital part in influencing children's attitudes to learning. Where a parent chooses to employ a nanny, this person becomes the children's carer when the parent is not present and as such plays a large part in providing for the informal education that takes place in the home.

It is very important for your nanny to plan learning activities, such as reading, singing, enjoying rhymes and going to the library, as children benefit enormously from these early language experiences. Conversation is important for babies and children and it is never too early for you and your nanny to start! The nanny needs to be aware of the importance of early learning activities and to plan activities that are appropriate for the age and stage of development of the children.

ACTIVITIES YOUR NANNY SHOULD REGULARLY CARRY OUT

- Reading to and with children
- Singing songs and enjoying rhymes with children
- Taking children on visits
- Enjoying painting and drawing activities
- Inviting the children's friends home to play
- Going to the library
- Having fun playing with letters and numbers in simple games and everyday activities

Your nanny should frequently carry out all of the above activities as there is evidence that such childcare promotes children's cognitive and social development skills and that these beneficial gains continue as children progress through school. A qualified nanny's training will have covered the importance of these activities, but it is the responsibility of the parents to ensure that their children have the opportunity to take part in them and to prompt their nanny if they do not. Discuss the day's events with your children and nanny to see what activities were enjoyed. Usually there is no problem as most nannies enjoy carrying out these activities with children.

CHILDREN ARE ACTIVE LEARNERS – CAN YOUR NANNY COPE?

A nanny needs to have an understanding of how children learn. Young children are active learners and have boundless energy and enthusiasm to learn and to take part in activities that interest and involve them. Their nanny also needs to have boundless energy and parents will do well to choose someone who looks as though he or she is an active and energetic person. Where nannies play a full part in supporting children's learning they will have tremendous job satisfaction in seeing how the children develop and know that they are meeting their employer's expectations in this regard.

THE IMPORTANCE OF PLAY

A nanny needs to ensure that your child has frequent, regular opportunities to play. Play is the foundation for all future learning and is a crucial part of the way in which a child's development is promoted. The ways in which children play differs from culture to culture and also happens in various ways in different families. For children to play in a happy and beneficial way there does not need to be a vast range of expensive toys but there does need to be a knowledgeable, enthusiastic nanny and/or parent who can 'tune into' children's interests. A nanny will be familiar with the scenario of the cardboard box that protects an expensive toy holding more interest for the child than the toy. This is because the box can be used in many different ways by imaginative children and supports their play in exactly the way children want. For example, on one occasion the box may be a nest and on another it may be the container for golden beans!

A nanny who can 'tune into' children, anticipate and follow their lead in play is a person who can be a teacher but also a play companion. It is important to understand that play does not have an outcome – something does not need to be made – rather it is a valuable learning experience in its own right. It is the processes of play that are important as children enjoy their experiences, organise their own games and rules and learn to cooperate and negotiate with their friends.

During play, children are active learners; they use their senses to explore and experiment, especially if they can have many first-hand experiences with natural materials and household objects. As they get older they represent these experiences through writing, drawing, modelling, dancing and other creative activities. When a nanny can organise and support play for the benefit of the children, parents will know that they have made a good choice of nanny.

THE ROLE OF THE NANNY IN CHILDREN'S LEARNING THROUGH PLAY IS TO:

- Provide a safe environment for play
- Understand the importance of play in promoting children's development
- Ensure that children have time and space to play on a regular basis
- Organise 'open-ended' materials and resources for play
- Follow the children's interests, being a play companion when invited to do so
- When appropriate, introduce new ideas and teach new skills
- Invite other children to join in play activities
- Share with parents the activities of their children

Children who are encouraged by their nanny to play are likely to become confident learners. They will gain a good foundation of knowledge and skills and develop attitudes to learning and new experiences that will be very helpful to them in later life. They will be able to:

- act independently
- confidently make choices
- try things out
- take appropriate risks in their learning
- understand that making mistakes is part of learning
- explore and carry out their own creative ideas
- invent their own play ideas
- feel proud of their achievements
- play with other children in a helpful and cooperative manner.

HOME-LEARNING AND YOUR NANNY
THE HOME-LEARNING ENVIRONMENT

Learning takes place in many different places – not just in the home. However, young children spend much of their time at home with their nanny and should have the opportunity to enjoy and make the best of everyday home activities. When the environment is right most children will naturally play and learn. Babies and young children learn best when they are well and are happy in familiar surroundings and with their nanny whom they know well. Books and simple materials, such as pencils, thick crayons, paper, glue, paint and cardboard boxes, provide the starting point for a whole range of creative activities. If your nanny is imaginative and resourceful then the children will enjoy and learn from the many ideas that are suggested. There is no particular need for expensive toys, which are often marketed with an 'excellent for learning' label.

If you need good ideas for birthday presents, discuss this with your nanny who should be able to make suggestions suitable for the children's age and stage of development. Toys that are open-ended and flexible in their use mean that the children can use them for an endless range of play purposes and will enjoy them for many years. Toys in this category include many construction toys, such as wooden bricks, Lego™ and Duplo™. It is essential that any toys purchased are absolutely safe, particularly for babies who can swallow small parts. Your nanny must be very aware of safety issues when there are older brothers or sisters in a family using a wide range of toys and a baby crawling or a toddler making rapid progress with walking. Ask your nanny how the safety of the baby or toddler is ensured.

YOUR NANNY SHOULD CREATE AN ENJOYABLE HOME-LEARNING ENVIRONMENT BY PROVIDING:

- A safe environment with space to play and enjoy a variety of activities
- Time for uninterrupted play
- Toys that are cleaned and repaired on a regular basis
- Toys and creative equipment suitable for the ages of the children in the family
- Special places for the children's toys – containers are useful to encourage the children to tidy away
- A particular place where 'work in progress' models and pictures can be safely left for a short time
- Toys and equipment that children can use in imaginative ways and for 'let's pretend' games
- A 'junk' box with modelling materials, such as empty cereal boxes and cardboard tubes
- A 'dressing-up' box with large pieces of material, unwanted hats, magic wands, bags and shoes
- A place, such as the kitchen table, which can be protected and used for messy play
- Regular opportunities to play with water and sand
- Opportunities for children to run, jump and play outside in the garden or the park

109

EVERYDAY ACTIVITIES

Good early years practice ensures that children have many first-hand practical experiences on which to base later learning. A nanny's job description will normally describe various domestic duties connected with the care of the children. The majority of these duties can be turned into enjoyable learning activities by a resourceful, inventive nanny; where the children are old enough they can join in and 'help' the nanny. Of course, these activities are likely to take longer with the children's help but they are an important part of the daily routine and will leave the children feeling very satisfied and immensely proud.

The following are good examples of home-learning experiences for young children:

Laundry
Your nanny should encourage the children to assist with taking out the washing from the washing machine as this can involve learning the names of articles of clothing, matching socks, learning colour names and counting.

Shopping
This also provides a wealth of learning opportunities. The journey to the shop enables children to recognise letters and numbers in lots of different environments. A nanny can help children to recognise the letters that are in their own name, to recognise logos and famous brand names. These are some of the first steps in learning to read. When children are helped to know what letters and words represent they are on the exciting path towards reading. This need not be a tortuous process but one that happens in a gradual, enjoyable way for children who are guided by an informed nanny.

True life stories: Fruit of knowledge

Raijii had looked after James and Joseph for over three years and knew that one of the boys' favourite activities was going to the supermarket. The children had a lively, inquisitive approach to everything they did and so Raijii kept them busy on the way to the supermarket by playing at spotting letters and words in the various road names, shapes on the road signs and letters and numbers on car registration plates. Shopping with the boys took longer than usual but was great fun. The fruit and vegetable section contained a lot of interest, as the boys liked to identify unusual specimens and discuss the country of origin of the item. The shopping trip also provided an opportunity to learn about colour, shape and money. Helping to put the shopping out ready for the checkout was the bit the boys enjoyed the most. Raiju knew that the shopping trip was beneficial as he listened to the boys recounting their 'adventures' to their parents.

Cooking

An excellent learning activity and one that is usually enjoyed by young children and their nanny is cooking. The nanny should choose a recipe that is simple and one where the children can do most of the activity. Not all cooking requires an oven. It is important for the nanny to be very aware of the safety issues in cooking. The use of knives should be closely supervised or, in some instances, carried out by the nanny who should always teach and demonstrate the safe use of knives. This is in itself a learning opportunity. The nanny should also help the children to get into the right habits from the start and explain to them the reasons for hand-washing prior to cooking, clearing up and being prepared to try and taste new foods.

A nanny should be aware of the learning that can take place from a cooking activity, including extending language and vocabulary and learning about the different countries connected with food. There will be many opportunities for the children to measure and count and learn about nutritious foods and the important part they play in growth and development. However, the most important ingredients in this learning activity will be the child and the nanny!

Inviting friends over for tea

This is an activity that children not only enjoy and look forward to but one from which they can also learn a great deal. Your nanny will need to be organised, resourceful and capable of coping with two or three children at the same time.

Having friends to visit can help teach children to be sociable and share toys, books and games. Children can also learn simple board games, such as 'snakes and ladders', which involves reading or listening to the directions, counting, tracking the counter up ladders and down snakes, following instructions, and learning about winning at some points and losing at others. As well as enjoying the games, the children could help prepare a simple tea such as eggy bread, flapjacks and fruit.

Children enjoy theme-based activities and these can often form the starting point for new interests. Younger children might enjoy activities and tea based on a colour. For older children, the visit could have a theme such as 'animals', with games and afternoon tea based on a favourite animal. Another visit could be centred round a forthcoming family holiday, providing plenty of opportunities to find out about different countries, their foods and songs. An inventive nanny could even set up a 'travel agents' for the afternoon play. Your nanny needs to be creative, energetic, enthusiastic and devote her energies to the afternoon's entertainment.

THE ROLE OF THE NANNY IN ENCOURAGING CHILDREN'S LANGUAGE DEVELOPMENT

Oral language skills are key factors in enabling children to read. Talking and, most importantly, listening are skills that precede reading. Nannies do not need to teach children how to talk as first language skills are naturally acquired when there is everyday, frequent conversation in the family setting. However, nannies do need to be good role models.

A nanny needs to talk, sing and read stories for babies as well as young children. Where there is conversation and storytelling, children will develop their first language skills at a truly phenomenal rate. It is never too early to start. Parents spending time at home should observe their nanny working and playing with the children to check that there is lots of conversation. This should also be the case for nannies working with babies. When care activities such as feeding, bathing or nappy changing are taking place, a caring and nurturing nanny will be providing the baby with a running commentary about what is happening. Babies will respond positively to the nanny's voice and enjoy the warm interaction and the opportunity to play games such as 'Round and round the garden' and 'Peekaboo'.

The importance of storytelling, reading and singing cannot be over emphasised. Children who are deprived of these daily activities are at a disadvantage in extending their language development. Your nanny should enjoy these activities and your children should be able to share their knowledge of songs and stories with you.

Songs and action rhymes

As children get older they can join their nanny in singing action rhymes, such as 'Wind the bobbin up' and 'Peter has one hammer'. Very often children join in with the actions first, then with a few words that are frequently repeated. Soon they master the whole rhyme and ask for it to be repeated endlessly! A competent nanny should have an extensive repertoire of songs and action rhymes.

Reading and storyelling

Make sure that you have provided lots of books for your nanny and your baby; these should include sensory touch books, lift-the-flap books, as well as picture and board book versions of much-loved children's stories, such as *We're Going on a Bear Hunt* by Michael Rosen. A nanny's knowledge should also extend to knowing which stories will be enjoyed by children of particular ages. Parents should be able to ask their nanny for particular recommendations of books. Stories are not just for bedtime, and should be read by the nanny throughout the day.

Children enjoy variety: having some stories read to them and at other times stories told to them. They enjoy it especially when stories are made up with them as the central character. Children also like stories to be repeated with a central character who has many different adventures.

PREPARING CHILDREN FOR SCHOOL

Preparing children for school is a key role for your nanny, who should enable children to gain the most from their experiences and ensure that they enjoy their time in school. Most children now benefit from some form of early years education before starting formal schooling after their fifth birthday. This early years experience can be a combination of being looked after by a nanny and attending a pre-school or nursery school on a part-time basis.

Children who have a nanny will often be used to being away from their parents for significant periods of time, yet they will still need to be introduced gradually to the new routine of school. Children who are the oldest in the family will be the pathfinders and may need some considerable support from their nanny, but they will, in time, help their younger siblings when it is their turn to start school.

Choosing which school to attend has to be a parent's decision but your nanny can play an important role in supporting you in the preparation of the children in starting school. A positive approach by everyone is essential and everybody needs to adopt the approach that school is a place where many new friends will be found and new experiences enjoyed. The school will probably have some visiting times prior to the formal start date. Make sure that your children visit the school and meet their teacher. If your nanny is taking the children, make a list of the helpful things that need to be found out, such as the usual daily routine, lunch arrangements and if there is any special uniform worn for games lessons. Parents will have been notified of any requirements for school uniform. Children sometimes worry about things that may seem to be unimportant to an adult but have great significance for them: they need to know where the toilets are, whether they are having a school dinner or a packed lunch and who will be collecting them from school. Most parents worry about their child being intellectually ready for school, however, it is important for children to be socially ready for school, able to make new friends and have

HOW YOUR NANNY CAN ENCOURAGE INDEPENDENCE IN YOUR CHILDREN

Before attending full-time school, your nanny should make sure your children are able to:

- Take themselves to the toilet and be confident to ask the teacher in plenty of time
- Have the ability to express their needs and wishes
- Put on their shoes, coat and hat and, if possible, gloves or mittens
- Undress and dress for games lessons
- Be confident to play with other children in the playground
- Be confident to ask questions and to talk with adults in their classroom
- Sit still for a short period of time and to listen carefully
- Follow simple instructions
- Look after themselves at mealtimes
- Take appropriate responsibility for their belongings

developed skills in looking after themselves. Your nanny can be a great support in these areas.

Many children who have enjoyed simple numeracy and literacy games and activities at home with their nanny will be able to recognise some letters and numbers and hopefully their name. Knowing how their name is written is a very useful skill for children starting school as they will then be able to recognise named articles of clothing, their named book bag and sometimes their name card indicating where their lunch place is.

There are certain attitudes to learning that enable children to develop as confident, autonomous learners. A competent nanny can encourage these skills as both children and nanny take part in simple learning activities in the home environment. For example, children need to be offered the opportunity to try new things and not to worry when things do not go exactly to plan. Children who are able to approach activities in school with a positive and independent approach are ready to learn and to enjoy being at school. They have an excellent foundation on which to build and are likely to make good progress. When parents and nannies can work together in this way the children will certainly benefit.

ENCOURAGING PLAY AND LEARNING

Learning activities organised by a nanny do not need to be very complicated. Hopefully your nanny will arrive with a large 'Mary Poppins' type bag containing a wealth of materials and a huge range of exciting ideas. Understandably, a parent may be asked to fund the raw materials, such as paper, card, glue, sequins and feathers, but these are the tools of the trade and are necessary for your nanny to carry out her role. As already mentioned, play does not always have to have an end product but you should occasionally be able to see some signs of your children's creativity as they will enjoy making various things to show you. Children's models, pictures and drawings do not need to be easily recognisable by an adult. Most children feel very proud of their efforts and may want to tell you about their creations. Try not to say, 'What is it?' but rather 'Tell me about your colourful picture'. In this way you are less likely to find yourself in a very involved discussion about what you thought was an ostrich but which turned out to be a picture of you!

Children like knowing when their birthday is and look forward to the time when it can be celebrated. A nanny can use this interest for the child to learn the names of the months and to count. An enjoyable creative activity that could be organised by your nanny is to make a train with 12 carriages and to name each carriage with the name of the month. Then draw some people to put into the carriage or some faces in the carriage windows according to when each member of the family has his or her birthday. The children could also find out when their friends' birthdays are and place them accordingly. This type of activity needs to be stored safely or put up in the child's bedroom or the nursery playroom ready for working out when to celebrate birthdays. Your nanny should have ideas such as these in abundance!

Many excellent children's stories are the basis for their learning. For example, your nanny should know of Eric Carle's *The Very Hungry Caterpillar* and the learning that can come through this story. From the activities of the Hungry Caterpillar children can learn about the days of the week and some familiar and less familiar foods, such as apples, pears, plums, salami, pickle and watermelon. Children can also enjoy discussing with their nanny their favourite and not so favourite foods. A competent nanny uses stories and play activities as the basis for a wealth of learning activities.

True life stories: Boys' toys

Matthew, aged three, was very interested in cars. His nanny, Elspeth, made sure that Matthew had the opportunity to regularly play with his cars and garage at home. Matthew knew the colours and brand names of many of his cars and Elspeth would point out some well-known makes of cars when they were on their way to the shops. She soon noticed that Matthew then did this for her! On some occasions Matthew's friend Dominic and his nanny came to play. Both nannies encouraged their charges to share the cars and to take turns in placing the cars in the garage. The boys had many 'car' conversations and enjoyed each other's company. When Matthew's father came home in the evening Matthew recounted the day's events clearly and with evident enjoyment.

CHAPTER 8

SPECIALIST NANNIES FOR SPECIAL SITUATIONS

All families are different. A nanny who is able to assist parents in bringing up children to be happy and contented within a particular and possibly unusual family situation is likely to have a special expertise, be an experienced practitioner and an adaptable, sensitive person.

Whatever the special family situation, the requirements of the job need to be clearly stated on the job description and fully discussed at interview. It would be ideal if the potential nanny had a relevant qualification and extensive experience but if the nanny appears to be adaptable, flexible and open minded, this is a good start.

In this chapter, some special family situations will be considered and guidance given as to some of the points to consider when employing a nanny in these circumstances.

- *Employing a maternity nurse*
- *Nannies for children with special needs*
- *Travelling abroad with young children*
- *Bringing up children bilingually*
- *Supporting children who are bereaved*
- *Nannies for gifted and talented children*

EMPLOYING A MATERNITY NURSE

Many parents choose to employ an experienced nanny as a maternity nurse for their first baby, or for subsequent babies if they wish they had employed a maternity nurse the first time! Generally, the responsibilities of a maternity nurse will cover all aspects of caring for the newborn and supporting the mother in the first few weeks after the birth. Many agencies specialise in the placement of maternity nurses, who will work extremely hard in those first weeks of the baby's life.

WHAT SHOULD YOU PAY YOUR MATERNITY NURSE?

Parents need to be prepared to pay a premium rate for a maternity nurse, particularly if he or she is very experienced. Trained and experienced maternity nurses are highly sought after, tend to be 'passed around' by word of mouth, and rarely have to look for work. They are booked up months in advance, so don't leave your search to the last minute. As soon as you know you are pregnant, start looking!

Some parents employ a maternity nurse before the baby is born. This ensures that the nurse you want will be available at the right time, even if it means having to pay an extra week's salary or, if a longer period is involved, some maternity nurses will agree to a 50 per cent weekly rate. During the 'waiting weeks', the maternity nurse may agree to undertake a few outstanding preparatory tasks for the nursery. He or she is usually happy to give advice on the essential baby equipment and can save parents money by saying what is really required and what are non-essential luxuries. Please note that maternity nurses caring for twins and triplets earn more.

As usual, parents are advised to give careful thought to the duties and the job description, as maternity nurses tend to have a very clear idea of what their duties will be and will not wish to stray too far from their own views. They expect to be on duty for 24 hours a day, six days a week. One day off each week is a definite and understandable requirement! They will sleep when the baby sleeps and will expect to get up at night to feed any baby who is bottle-fed. Many maternity nurses will also sleep in the same room as the baby and bring the baby to the mother for breastfeeding and then change and settle the baby back to sleep.

INTERVIEWING FOR A MATERNITY NURSE

When interviewing for a prospective maternity nurse, find out the candidates' views on breast- and bottle-feeding, as you will want to employ someone who will support you in whatever decision you make and not force his or her views on you or give you feelings of guilt if your view is different from his or hers. Discuss the fact that you may wish to see your baby at any time of the day or night and will do so when you want to. You may want to use a baby-monitoring device or a particular type of nappy; it is your choice to care for your baby as you wish, and your maternity nurse needs to be able to accommodate your wishes and advise you. Most maternity nurses are flexible, but there are some who have very definite ideas of their own and can make parents feel as though their home has been taken over. Of course, if this is what you want then appoint accordingly, but be alert as to what type of person you are interviewing.

Other points to discuss at the interview could include asking about previous experiences and emergencies that have been dealt with. You may want to know what type of routine may be recommended for your baby or how successful breastfeeding can be established. In all of the answers to your questions look for warmth, a desire to be supportive and a genuine interest in each baby's individual needs. There should not be a 'one size fits all' approach.

True life stories: Off to a good start

Claire the maternity nurse arrived the day before Emily was born. She exuded professionalism and a calmness that Helen and Lee found very reassuring. When Helen and Emily arrived home from the birthing centre, everything was organised for them. Although the nursery was ready, Claire was sensitive to Helen wanting Emily to be near her so put Emily into the crib close to Helen. Claire supported Helen by giving her advice about breastfeeding and encouraged her to persevere at the times when, due to tiredness and difficulty with Emily 'latching on', she did feel tempted to give up. Over the next few weeks Claire helped with night-time feeds, taught Helen how to bath Emily and dealt with all of her laundry.

A particular skill that Claire had was the ability to include Lee in all ways possible related to Emily's care. She established a routine that meant that Helen could have some rest during the day and was happy to prepare lunch for Helen at whatever time suited her. Claire was happy to share her knowledge and experience in such a way that Helen never felt undermined, and she was as ready as she could be to take over the reins when Claire departed six weeks after Emily was born. Helen felt that she had been well supported and given a good start to continue the excellent routine that she had established with Claire's expert help.

WHAT ARE THE RESPONSIBILITIES OF A MATERNITY NURSE?

Many first-time parents think that employing a maternity nanny is well worth the money. They list the benefits as follows:

- Learning more about feeding, both bottle-feeding and breastfeeding
- Feeling supported and more relaxed
- Having time to recover from the birth
- Learning new skills, such as bathing and nappy changing
- Knowing what do to when their baby cries
- Having a routine established
- Getting a better night's sleep
- Dealing with a constant stream of visitors
- Getting some advice on baby equipment
- Feeling more confident and developing coping strategies
- Learning how new fathers can best support their partners

NANNIES FOR CHILDREN WITH SPECIAL NEEDS

Working parents of children who have special needs can find themselves in very challenging circumstances. They frequently need to make appointments to discuss their children's circumstances with health and education specialists and find that their time and energy are very much at a premium. Employing a nanny can give not only them but all of the family much-needed support.

Many qualified nannies wish to work with children who have special needs. They may have gained good experience working with children who have normal development and wish to broaden their experience by working in this specialised field. All children are special but there are some who need to be cared for by nannies who are very skilled and sensitive. Important factors in the choice of nanny are for parents to feel able to totally trust the person and to be willing to share their knowledge of their own child. The parents may need to help the nanny to acquire certain necessary skills, perhaps through an extended induction or handover period. The time and effort put in by parents at this stage will be amply rewarded in the future.

WHAT ARE 'SPECIAL NEEDS'?

'Special needs' refers to children whose development differs in some way from the normal stages of development. However, when choosing a nanny to work with children with special needs, it is important to employ someone who is able to respond to the individual needs of the child. The nanny needs to see the child first and his or her special need or disability second. Some agencies specialise in placing nannies wishing to work with children who have special needs and parents would be advised to contact such agencies, as they will not only have suitable nannies on their books but should also be able to support parents in the recruitment process.

Children with special needs still have the same needs as children with normal development, including love, stability, security and protection, but they are more vulnerable. If at all possible, they need a nanny who will stay with the family for a prolonged period of time as such children often find frequent changes of nannies very unsettling. Parents should discuss this at interview and, while no one can predict what they will be doing in a few years' time, it is as well to rule out anybody who has clearly made plans to be in a different place in six months' time.

Very often the child's special educational need will have been identified by his or her nursery school or pre-school. Occasionally, it will have been identified as a possible area of concern by the child's parents or nanny and is confirmed by staff at the child's school. A child with a special educational need may have a learning difficulty that needs special teaching and professional support: sometimes this is due to a sensory impairment resulting in a hearing loss or sight deficiency; at other times the child's difficulty in learning is due to a speech or language impairment or a behavioural problem that requires both social and emotional support. If a parent or nanny has any concerns about the child's progress he or she should discuss it and take advice from the appropriate health or education professional. Early identification and intervention is in the best interests of the child.

CARING FOR CHILDREN WHO HAVE DISABILITIES

When interviewing a nanny to work with a child who has a disability look for someone who will be sensitive to the situation but have clear boundaries for the child, just as with other children. A skilful nanny will be able to work closely with parents to tread the fine line between being protective yet encouraging as much independence and self-reliance as possible. The role of the nanny in this situation is not only to work with the child but also with any other professional workers involved in the child's care and development. An important part of the job is to keep parents regularly and reliably informed of the child's progress and the plans put in place by any other members of the professional team.

THE PERFECT NANNY FOR A CHILD WITH A DISABILITY

Look to appoint a nanny who:
- Has the knowledge and skills to manage the child's disability in a sensitive and skilful manner
- Promotes a positive self-image in the child
- Has patience and good communication skills
- Works in a manner that shows respect and maintains the child's dignity
- Gives as much freedom of choice and independence to the child as is possible
- Has a positive approach to the child's disability
- Gives the child appropriate responsibility, helping others when possible
- Supports the child's integration into nursery, pre-school or formal schooling
- Understands the need to give the child justified praise for effort as well as achievement
- Acts as a good role model
- Genuinely enjoys the work and gains job satisfaction from dealing with the challenges

WORKING WITH CHILDREN WHO HAVE SPECIAL EDUCATIONAL NEEDS

The government's programme 'Every Child Matters: Change for Children' created a new environment for the care of children with special educational needs, with the emphasis on early identification, effective support and the better integration of professional services to support the children and their families. The programme's approach is to provide support that is coherent and structured and properly funded to achieve these aims.

As with all children, but particularly so with children who have special needs, a united and consistent approach by all adults caring for the child is essential. Since the 2001 Special Educational Needs Code of Practice, and depending on the child's age, there is a right for children to be educated in 'mainstream' schools and to be integrated and included with their peer group, if necessary with appropriate human and physical resources. Parents have a right to be given relevant advice and information and to be kept informed about the provision made for their child, if necessary with external support agencies. The nanny's role is to work within this framework, acting as an advocate for both the child and the family. An experienced nanny will be able to use professional skills in supporting parents in their dealings with various support agencies. This is a complex role and one requiring maturity as well as professional knowledge and skills.

Each child who needs extra help will have an individual action plan and very possibly a key worker to implement it. Close cooperation and good communication are key factors here. The nanny needs to be the constant link between the professionals, usually the key worker, and the parents.

Following the interview, try to think if the person you intend to appoint could not only work well with all members of the family but also has the experience to liaise on a professional basis with all of the people that you as the parent may have been working with in order for your child to make progress.

TRAVELLING ABROAD WITH YOUNG CHILDREN

Many families who frequently travel overseas do so because it is a requirement of one or both parents' work. These families employ a nanny to provide stability in their family life. Most children are easily adaptable to living in foreign countries and cultures when the aspects of their lives that are really important to them remain constant. Generally, these aspects are their close family members. Parents who are thinking of employing a nanny to accompany them on their frequent travels abroad need to find a very special sort of nanny who could become part of the family. The recruitment process, as always, is the key.

It is very important to make sure there are no surprises in store for the nanny once appointed. Employers need to be clear about what the job entails, stating how regularly the family is due to travel overseas and how long the stay is likely to be. The nanny also needs to know which countries are likely to be visited and the type of accommodation that the family will have. A note is needed in the job description if the nanny will be working for six days or more each week and if the stay will involve being 'on duty' or 'on call' for particular periods of time. Most overseas travel will involve many flights, possibly with long delays, and the nanny will be expected to be 'on duty' for all of this time.

Looking after young children overseas can be very demanding, and if the nanny is required to be available for babysitting due to the parents' evening engagements this must be made clear from the start. Parents should, however, recognise these additional duties by perhaps arranging some extra time 'off duty' for the nanny, perhaps when the family arrive home. During the interview, parents need to tread the fine line between being quite clear about what the job involves and making the job attractive for the right applicant.

WHAT SORT OF PERSON SHOULD PARENTS LOOK FOR?
There are particular qualities that a nanny needs for this type of job. Organisational skills top the list, along with adaptability and resourcefulness. Ideally, you want to employ someone who has demonstrated the ability to look after one's self abroad before taking

SUGGESTED INTERVIEW QUESTIONS

- Have you had much experience in travelling abroad?
- What countries have you visited?
- How long did each trip last?
- What did you particularly enjoy about your experiences?

- How do you cope with any difficulties experienced?
- What attracted you to this particular job?
- In which languages are you fluent?
- Do you have conversational skills in any other languages?

on the responsibility for young children in this situation. Your nanny needs to have a realistic idea of what is involved rather than some romantic notion of a glamorous life at the employer's expense.

If the very general questions at the foot of the last page seem to be heading in the right direction and you are discussing the job with someone who seems to enjoy travelling abroad and copes well with the unexpected, move on to more specific questions about travelling overseas with young children.

SUGGESTED SCENARIO QUESTIONS

• **'You will be responsible for all the packing for our young baby. How will you go about this?'**

Listen for answers that do not involve packing up the whole nursery on a 'just in case' basis. It is quite likely that on a long-haul flight there will be a luggage weight restriction and you will not want to find yourself paying for excess baggage.

In carry-on luggage a nanny should pack whatever clothes are needed for the flight and then some extra items to cope with delays or accidents. The clothes need to be worn in layers and easily removed in a confined space.

A baby will also need whatever food and drink is required according to his or her stage of development. It is much better to take some familiar food for the baby rather than to rely on what the airline offers. Food and drink, besides being a necessity, can provide distraction on long flights and for babies is an important means of relieving ear pressure through using the swallowing reflex during take-off and landing; a small cool bag is a useful item of hand luggage. Please note that some airport security restrictions insist that you can only take 100ml of fluid per container.

The nanny needs to be self-sufficient regarding sun hat, sun-protection cream, nappies, changing mat, bottles, bibs, wipes

continued on next page

and tissues. He or she needs to remember the buggy, as this is key to a successful exit from the airport when everyone has lots of items to carry. It is also very useful to have the buggy available between checking in and boarding. An experienced nanny would also add a small cot sheet and sleeping bag to the list to supplement what the airline provides in its on-board baby bassinets. This covers the eventuality of them not being available but also provides the baby with his or her own familiar belongings. Your nanny should suggest contacting the airline to see what is offered for a baby during the flight. For example, Gulf Air has invested in trained Sky Nannies to help parents care for their babies and young children on long-haul flights.

'How will you keep our four-year-old entertained during our travels?'

An inventive nanny will take a small selection of toys and books but also rely on activities that do not need a great deal of equipment and are designed not to be too noisy or disturbing to the other passengers. Making paper aeroplanes may seem a suitable activity until the child decides to give it a test flight in the confined space of the aircraft! A selection of books, paper and colouring pencils is a good start. Choose books that are the child's favourites as well as some entirely new ones. An experienced nanny may say that when the child is due to have a sleep that a book would be chosen to replicate the bedtime routine at home.

As well as these specific questions you will also want to know that the nanny has an up-to-date first-aid certificate and would be able to choose items for a small first-aid kit to take with the family. Above all, try to establish during the interview that you and your children would enjoy travelling with this person and that there is the likelihood that he or she could remain cheerful in the face of adversity!

When the first family trip has taken place, remember to discuss with your nanny the pros and cons and what could be learnt for the next trip. If you feel that the nanny worked hard and was supportive remember to tell him or her so and give any time off that was agreed.

HELPING THE NANNY STAY HAPPY

When nannies are abroad for long periods of time they often find that the ability to remain in contact with their family and friends is a vital part of remaining happy. Fortunately, the use of emailing and free phone calls using computer software such as Skype makes this relatively easy. It does, however, require the employer to make the necessary arrangements beforehand.

True life stories: Keeping in touch

Mr and Mrs G were pleased that Ellie had accepted their offer of employment. During the two interviews they had carefully explained the job role, ensuring that Ellie appreciated the fact that she would be living abroad with her airfare back to the UK paid for once a year. She was excited but also nervous about the new job. One of Ellie's concerns was that she would feel homesick. She did, however, want to widen her experience and thought that the job was a wonderful opportunity for her. A trial period of two months was agreed on both sides so that if either party was unhappy with the arrangement the contract could be terminated. Mrs G arranged for Ellie to have internet access in her accommodation; Ellie found this to be a lifeline, especially in the early stages of the employment. It enabled her to keep in contact with family and friends and to keep up with the news from home. As time passed, Ellie noticed that she reduced the time with her laptop, but knew that the ability to keep in touch was an important factor in settling into the job. She stayed with the family for nearly three years.

BRINGING UP CHILDREN BILINGUALLY

Many families wish to bring up their children to be bilingual. Some parents may not have English as their first language, and may use their mother tongue to converse with members of their family and English for all conversations outside the home. In this situation, they may wish their young children to learn English in the home through an English-speaking nanny as this will be the language used in their nursery or pre-school and formal schooling. On the other hand, English-speaking parents may wish to employ a nanny with a different first language in order to introduce a new language to their children.

When interviewing a nanny, parents should look for someone who understands that a young child can learn an additional language through play, songs, rhymes and the everyday activities that take place in the home environment. They need to employ a nanny who understands a young child's language development and knows the benefits of bringing up young children bilingually. It is important for parents to agree with their nanny a simple structure within which to work. This is usually that one or both parents continue to use the home language with the child and the nanny will use the second language. In this way the child is able to sort out who speaks each language and will reply using the language of the speaker.

It is very natural for young children in the early stages of bilingualism to sometimes use both languages in one sentence. For a young child this is the quickest way for them to communicate and should not be a cause for concern for parents. The child knows what he or she wants to say, understands the concept and just uses the vocabulary that first comes to mind. As proficiency in both languages improves, the child will acquire the vocabulary and language structures to be equally skilful in both languages.

THE BENEFITS OF BILINGUALISM

Young children who are brought up bilingually are able to learn not only more than one language but also learn about more than one culture. They appreciate not only the differences but also the similarities in various cultures. Children who are exposed to a language other than their first language do not become confused. Initially their progress in language development may appear to be slower than their monolingual peers but they quickly catch up, usually by the time they attend formal schooling.

HOW A NANNY CAN ENCOURAGE CHILDREN TO LEARN AN ADDITIONAL LANGUAGE

- Be certain to read and tell stories on a daily basis
- Choose picture books where the story content is of relevance and interest to the children
- Share action rhymes and songs with the children
- Understand that children will join in with the actions before joining in with the song
- Use everyday household activities as 'language development' opportunities
- Accept the children's use of their first language and take the opportunity to learn something of their language and culture
- Remember to give praise for the child's efforts
- Find out how children acquire their first language and use a similar approach
- Be careful not to exclude family members from conversations where they do not speak certain languages

When the childen's spoken languages are established they are ready to make progress with reading and writing. A nanny who has helped to promote the foundations of spoken English will have also helped the child to settle well into school and make friends.

Children who can communicate in two or more languages are well placed for the future. Over time, bilingual children will have greater future employment and study opportunities, especially when one of their languages is English. In addition, they will gain a developed understanding of what it means to be a global citizen.

SUPPORTING CHILDREN WHO ARE BEREAVED

In this situation, more than any other, children need support that is sensitive to their individual needs. A nanny taking up employment in a home where one of the parents has recently died will have to have the emotional maturity and experience to deal with some very difficult situations. There are both practical and emotional aspects for a nanny working in these challenging circumstances to consider, so it is important to employ someone who has already had some nanny experience and who has the emotional maturity and inner resilience to be sensitive to the turmoil that the child and the surviving partner are experiencing. Key aspects to be considered when employing a nanny in this very delicate situation include finding someone who will be able to give the child some security and stability while understanding that he or she may seem to be uncooperative with the very person who is trying to help them. The nanny will need to try to keep as close as possible to the child's daily routine and to continue to work closely with any school or pre-school staff who also work with the child. It will be helpful if the nanny has some agreed strategy with the parent as to how the inevitable questions will be answered.

Young children can find it very difficult to deal with any sort of separation and, as they do not have a real understanding of the concept of time, they may think that the person who has died will be 'coming back later'. Gradually and gently, the child needs to know that this is not the case. The best way to deal with situations of bereavement is to answer the child's questions truthfully, gauging the level of interest and understanding. Both the nanny and the parent should be prepared for the child's questions to be asked at any time and not always at the most convenient or appropriate time. In this case, the child may have to wait for an answer but the nanny should be sure to make time to discuss the child's questions and should not ignore them. Very often children will try to work out for themselves the answers to their questions through their play. An experienced nanny will closely observe the child and be ready to become involved in the play while not intervening as the child decides for himself the direction in which his play will evolve.

It is also possible that the child will dislike his or her nanny and only time, understanding and empathy will possibly improve the situation. The way the bereavement process will unfold and how long it lasts will depend on the age of the child. An experienced nanny will be prepared for this and may have to discuss with the child's parent if any outside professional help is required.

NANNIES FOR GIFTED AND TALENTED CHILDREN

Gifted and talented children are born into all sorts of families and their abilities may or may not be recognised before they begin formal schooling. They need support and encouragement to meet their individual needs, just like all children. If, as a parent, you are employing a nanny to work with your child who is talented or gifted, ensure that the nanny has sufficient energy, interest and ability to work successfully in this situation.

Children who are described as 'gifted' can have academically or artistically superior abilities over a wide range of interests. Children who are 'talented' may have a specific ability, such as in music, sport or dance. Frequently these children are very demanding and they need a nanny who understands their needs and can respond to them in a supportive and encouraging manner. Try to employ a nanny who shares a similar interest. The following areas are often the ones where young children can need particular support and where your nanny needs to have the capability, understanding and sensitivity to encourage the development of these abilities.

General characteristics of gifted and talented children include:

- Being a competent, fluent, early reader – in this case, your nanny needs to be able to support your child by choosing books that are at an appropriate reading level but importantly with content that is relevant and of interest to the child. Your nanny should still continue to read to your child and share all types of books including picture books and non-fiction books.
- Being very articulate – your nanny needs to able to enjoy far-ranging conversations and discussions. When questions are asked where the answer is not readily available, the nanny should find out the answer, including the child in the 'finding out' process, by perhaps visiting the library or looking at a relevant website. Your

child may enjoy being with and communicating with adults but it is important that your nanny supports and encourages your child to share experiences and play with his or her peer group.

- Having quick verbal responses – your nanny needs to understand that sometimes these immediate responses are not meant to appear 'cheeky' but your nanny should explain the boundaries of what is acceptable.
- Having a wide range of interests and general knowledge – where your child indicates that an interest needs to be further explored your nanny should be capable of doing this, enjoying the experience with your child. In this way your child can often teach himself and crucially it is a very motivating experience, as for young children the way in which adults encourage positive and enjoyable attitudes to learning is as important as the learning itself.
- Enjoying music, drawing and dancing – your nanny needs to encourage these talents, perhaps sharing aspects of these interests and taking your child to art galleries or theatre events that are organised for young children.
- Excelling at sport – your nanny will hopefully recognise if your child is physically very capable and coordinated. For very young children, an energetic nanny is needed, with plenty of active play and simple games played with friends and family. When your child is older, playing in a team or developing the talent outside the home may be the next step.

It is also very important for the nanny to make sure that a child who is gifted or talented is encouraged and supported to make friends and to enjoy sharing interests, playing and socialising with them. Sometimes gifted and talented children feel the need to hide their abilities as they do not wish to seem 'different'. Make certain that your nanny knows the importance of building your child's confidence and self-esteem and enables the child to know that being different is perfectly acceptable, while encouraging them to enjoy the social activities of their peer group.

SCENARIO INTERVIEW QUESTIONS

- Our four-year-old daughter has been identified by her pre-school teacher as gifted. What are your reasons for wanting to work with her?
- How do you think you could keep her interested in her reading and enjoyment of books?
- What sort of books do you think she might enjoy?
- We are keen for her to begin learning to write and to link this with her enjoyment of reading. How could you do this?
- We're very keen for her not to be seen by other children as 'different'. How would you make sure that this does not happen?
- Our daughter is very articulate and is always asking questions. How will you cope with this?
- What interests do you enjoy that you could share with our daughter?
- We are keen for her to take part in and enjoy some outdoor activities. How will you encourage this?

Many nannies who have several years' experience in working with children relish the challenge of working with 'special' children. If it is their first experience, they may need some extra help with settling in, and they will definitely need as much information about the particular circumstances in which they will be working. Experience is not everything, as everyone has to start somewhere. Search for a person who will fit in well with your family. Look for someone who seems adaptable and flexible and who has a calm, confident approach. Hopefully, that person will become your perfect nanny!

USEFUL SOURCES

The following organisations and websites are useful for finding additional detail and for ensuring that information is up to date.

FINDING YOUR WAY THROUGH THE CHILDCARE MAZE

ChildcareLink
www.childcarelink.gov.uk

Children's Information Service
www.childrensinformationservice.org.uk

Council for Awards in Children's Care and Education
www.cache.org.uk

Daycare Trust
www.daycaretrust.org.uk

Department for Children, Schools and Families
www.dcsf.gov.uk

National Childminding Association
www.ncma.org.uk

National Day Nurseries Association
www.ndna.org.uk

Pre-School Learning Alliance
www.pre-school.org.uk

Sure Start
www.surestart.gov.uk

THE NANNY SEARCH

The Chiltern College
www.chilterncollege.com

The Lady
www.lady.co.uk

Nanny Nanny
www.nanny-nanny.co.uk

NannyPlus Childcare Ltd
www.nannyplus.co.uk

Norland College
www.norland.co.uk

Nursery World
www.nurseryworld.co.uk

EMPLOYER RESPONSIBILITIES

Child Accident Prevention Trust
www.capt.org.uk

Directgov (parental employment rights and guidance)
www.direct.gov.uk

HM Revenue and Customs
www.hmrc.gov.uk

Nanny Tax
www.nannytax.co.uk

PAYE for Nannies
www.payefornannies.co.uk

The Recruitment & Employment Confederation
www.rec.uk.com

EARLY YEARS EDUCATION IN THE HOME

Bookstart (free books for children)
www.bookstart.co.uk

Early Years Educator
www.earlyyearseducator.co.uk

Office for Standards in Education
www.ofsted.gov.uk

Parents, Early Years and Learning
www.peal.org

SPECIALIST NANNIES FOR SPECIAL SITUATIONS

Contact a Family (services for children with a disability)
www.cafamily.org.uk

Early Support (services for children with disability)
www.earlysupport.org.uk

MISCELLANEOUS

ACAS   (information on employment disputes)
www.acas.org.uk

The Family and Parenting Institute
www.familyandparenting.org

ForParentsByParents
www.forparentsbyparents.com

National Childbirth Trust
www.nctpregnancyandbabycare.com

ParentsCentre
www.parentscentre.gov.uk

Working Families
www.workingfamilies.org.uk

INDEX

A

accommodation: for resident nanny 59, 74
action rhymes 113
activities: for children 105
agencies:
    au pair 22
    checks carried out by 44, 73
    code of practice 37
    feedback to 73
    registering with 66
    for special needs 122
    using 36-8
aggression 92
allergies: food 75
animals in home 40
appraisal 85
au pairs 22–4
    definition 23

B

bereavement: supporting children in 131–3
bilingualism 129–31
    benefits of 130–1
birthdays:
    knowing dates of 116–17
    presents for children 108
books 113
BTEC Diploma 33

C

CACHE *see* Council for Awards in Children's Care and Education
cars: use by nanny 75, 81
certificates 31–2
Child Tax Credit (CTC) 14
childcare:
    accessibility 16
    affordability 13–14
    alternatives to employing nanny 16–24
    availability 11
    certificate of 16
    checks on 15
    family needs 8–11
    inspections 15
    priorities 9
    quality of 12
    registered 14–16
    types 6
Childcare Vouchers 14, 68–9
childcarers:
    checking 11
    interaction with children 12
childminders 6, 21–2
    registered 15
children:
    aggression in 92
    bereaved 131–3
    bilingual 129–31
    birthday presents 108

139

development: knowledge of 91–2
gifted 133–5
independence: encouraging 115
language development 112–13
learning: help from nanny 105–14
listening to 89-90
managing behaviour of 91–3
preparing for new nanny 63, 76
preparing for school 114–16
reactions to nanny 89–90
role in choosing nanny 61
sanctions 91
special needs: nannies for 122–5
talented 133–5
children's centres 17, 18–19
Children's Information Service 11
Chiltern Certificate 34
cognitive development 105
communication 85–8, 90
contracts:
drawn up and signed 97
of employment 70–1
psychological 95–7
conversation 105
cooking:
for children 75
children helping with 111
Council for Awards in Children's Care and Education (CACHE):
guidelines 12–13
qualifications 32
checking 65

Criminal Records Bureau (CRB) 15, 21, 65
CVs 66
scrutinising 44–5

D
day nurseries 6, 17–18
diary: family 87–8, 93
Diplomas 31–2
disabilites, children with 123–5
perfect nanny for 124
dress code 28, 81–2

E
education:
early years 11, 114
further: for nanny 102–3
in home 104–17
Effective Provision of Pre-School Education (EPPE) 104
employers:
ground rules 46–8
responsibilities 64–71
'Every Child Matters; Change for Children' 124
expenses:
allowable 71
interview 44, 61

F
family:
changes in: discussing with nanny 101
childcare needs 8–11
choosing 95
nuclear 9
special requirements 40
family diary 87–8, 93

first aid:
   certificates 65
   experience in 128
food:
   allergies to 75
   preparation 75
formal arrangements 27–8
friends: inviting for tea 111–12
From Cradle to Crown 7

G
gifted children 133–5
government: national strategy 11
ground rules 46-8
Guardian Angels 66

H
HM Revenue and Customs (HMRC):
   registering with 66
   Tax Credit Helpline 13
holidays 100
   payment during 68
home:
   activities in 108–12
   education in 104–17
   learning environment 108-9
honesty 102
household matters 82–3

I
informal arrangements 27
information: important: list of 86
insurance 69
interviews 42–63
   areas for discussion 43
   by parents jointly 49, 50

candidate's questions 55–7
checklist 45–6
employer ground rules 46–8
first 49–57
   ending 56
   shortlisting after 57–8
making decision after 61–3
for maternity nurse 120
paying expenses for 44, 61
place for 48–9
pre-interview checks 44
preparing for 43–9
questions to ask 50–4
second 58–61
   reasons for 59
for travel abroad 126, 127–8

J
job description:
   example 40–1
   writing 38–41

L
The Lady 36
language:
   bilingualism 129–31
   encouraging development 112–13
   inadequate: causing tantrums 91–2
laundry: children helping with 110
learning:
   active 106, 107
   confidence in 107–8
   encouraging 116–17
   everyday activities 109–12
   help given by nanny 104–8
   home environment 108–12

nanny's role 107
  through play 106–8
local authorities: Children's
Information Service 11
loyalty 101

M
male nannies 6
maternity nurse:
  employing 119–21
  interviewing 120
  pay for 119–20
  responsibilities 121
mealtimes 80
'Meeting the Childcare
  Challenge' 11

N
nannies:
  appraisal of work 85
  carrying out checks on 65–6
  childcare alternatives to
    16–24
  children's reactions to 89–90
  choosing family 95
  communication with 85-8,
    90
  contract 70–1, 97
  CV 44–5, 66
  day or residential 24
  developing role 102–3
  discussions with 97
  dress code 28, 81–2
  employers' responsibilities
    64–71
  expectations of 95–100
  extending experience 103
  formal arrangements 27–8
  further education 102–3

giving feedback to 84–5
helping children learn
  105–13, 116–17
hours worked 25
informal arrangements 27
interviewing 42–63
male 6
management 72–93
meeting predecessor 60
non-registered 14
personal qualities 29–30
perspective of 94–103
'poaching' 36
preparing children for
  school 114–16
professional skills 34–5
psychological contract 95–7
reasons for employing 6
references 37–8, 61
relationship with 27, 72,
  101–2
  establishing 78
  managing 83–90
resident:
  accommodation for 59, 74
  additional costs 98
  drawbacks 83–4
  interviewing 58–9
  professional: maintaining
    88
role 27–31
search for 25–41
service provided 24–5
sharing care with parents
  29
sole charge 28–9
specialist 118–35
travel abroad 125–9
types 27–31

use of car 75, 81
welcoming 73–6
    checklist 77
    first week 77–83
    working with parents 77–8
nanny share 66–7
Nanny Tax 66
National Childcare Strategy
    11–12
National Day Nurseries
    Association 18
National Insurance 66, 67
National Nursery Examination
    Board: qualifications 32
Norland College 77
    Diploma 33–4
nurseries 14
    registered 15
nursery classes 19
nursery nursing: qualifications
    33, 34
nursery schools 17, 19
Nursery World 36
NVQs (National Vocational
    Qualifications) 33

O
off-duty time 100
Ofsted:
    checks carried out by 15,
        19, 20, 21
    Childcare Register (OCR)
        15, 65
    registered childcare 15-16
    voluntary registration 15,
        24, 65
Open University 103
out-of-school childcare 17, 20–1

P
parents:
    partnerships with 16
    sharing care with nanny 29
    support for 11–14
    working with nanny 77–8
pay 66-7, 97–8
    arrangements for 82
    going rate 70
    maternity pay 68
    sick pay 67
PAYE for Nannies 66
payslips 66
perks 99
person specification 43–4
personal qualities 29–30
pets 40
play:
    encouraging 116–17
    importance of 106-8
'poaching' nannies 36
pre-schools 14, 17, 20
professional skills 34–5
punctuality 81

Q
qualifications:
    checking 65
    early years 31–4
    Level 3 courses 31–4

R
reading 112, 113
Recruitment and Employment
    Confederation (REC) 36–7
references 37–8
    following up 61
registration:
    certificate of 16

INDEX

of childcare 14–16
of nurseries 15
relationship with nanny 27, 72,
101–2
establishing 78
long-lasting 101–2
managing 83–90
professional: maintaining
88–9
respect 101

S
safety 109
salary 97–8
going rate 70
paying 82
payment 66–7
salary sacrifice scheme 69
school:
choosing 114
preparing children for
114–16
shared care 29
shopping: children helping with
110–11
shortlisting 57–8
sick pay 67
singing 112, 113
social development 105
socialising 87
sole charge 28–9
Special Educational Needs
Code of Practice 124–5
special needs children:
care of 25
definition 122
educational difficulties 123,
124–5
nannies for 122–5

staff: defining roles of 27, 78
Statutory Maternity Pay (SMP)
68
Statutory Sick Pay (SSP) 67
storytelling 112, 113, 117

T
talented children 133–5
tantrums 91–2
tax 66–7
Ten Year Childcare Strategy 17
testimonials 37, 38
toys 108–9
travel abroad:
with children 125–9
interviewing nanny for 126,
127–8
keeping nanny happy 129
triplets: maternity nurse for 119
twins: maternity nurse for 119

U
uniform 28

W
Ward, Emily 77
weekly routine 78–83
working hours 99–100
Working Tax Credit (WTC)
13–14

Z
Zeepvat, Charlotte 7